D1405975

TOM & KIM BLACKABY

THE FAMILY GOD USES

LEAVING *A* LEGACY *OF* INFLUENCE

NEW HOPE
PUBLISHERS
BIRMINGHAM ALABAMA

New Hope® Publishers
P. O. Box 12065
Birmingham, AL 35202-2065
www.newhopepublishers.com
New Hope Publishers is a division of WMU®

Library of Congress Cataloging-in-Publication Data

Blackaby, Tom, 1962-
  The family God uses : leaving a legacy of influence / Tom and Kim Blackaby.
    p. cm.
  ISBN 978-1-59669-251-0 (jhc)
  1. Family--Religious aspects--Christianity. I. Blackaby, Kim, 1964-
II. Title.
  BV4526.3.B63 2009
  248.8'45--dc22

                                    2009021034

Scripture quotations marked NKJV are taken from the New King James Version. Copyright © 1982 by Thomas Nelson, Inc. Used by permission. All rights reserved.

Scripture quotations marked NIV are taken from the HOLY BIBLE, NEW INTERNATIONAL VERSION®. NIV®. Copyright©1973, 1978, 1984 by International Bible Society. Used by permission of Zondervan. All rights reserved.

Scripture quotations marked KJV are taken from The Holy Bible, King James Version.

Scripture quotations marked AMP are taken from the Amplified® Bible, Copyright © 1954, 1958, 1962, 1964, 1965, 1987 by The Lockman Foundation. Used by permission.

Scripture quotations marked GNT are from the Good News Translation—Second Edition © 1992 by American Bible Society. Used by Permission.

Scripture quotations marked NLT are taken from the *Holy Bible,* New Living Translation, copyright © 1996. Used by permission of Tyndale House Publishers, Inc., Wheaton, Illinois. All rights reserved.

Scripture quotations marked ASV are taken from The Holy Bible, American Standard Version.

Scripture quotations marked YLT are from *Young's Literal Translation.*

Creative Team: Joyce Dinkins, Sherry Hunt, Kathryne Solomon, Bruce Watford

Cover author photo credit: Amberlight Photography, Maple Ridge, Canada. Used by permission.

ISBN-10: 1-59669-251-0
ISBN-13: 978-1-59669-251-0
N104125 • 1009 • 10M1

DEDICATION

To our children, Erin, Matthew, and Conor

You have been a continual source of joy, blessing, fun, and wonder. You have challenged us to be better parents and better people. You have taught us more about ourselves and more about our God. We are forever grateful for the gift of you.

CONTENTS

Part 5: God Uses Children

Part 6: God's Invitation to Your Family

FOREWORD

HENRY T. BLACKABY

*F*rom eternity God planned—and purposed—the family. Each family is to be available to God for His purposes in their day and every person in a family is important to God. And each person in a family is to assist every other member of the family to know God intimately and respond to God's purposes. Therefore the standard and measure for each family is crucial, beginning with the father. God touched Abram and through him touched all the succeeding generations. For example, the covenant God made with Abram, He then made with Isaac (Genesis 22:15–18; 26:1–5). And so, throughout the rest of Scripture, God makes reference to "Abraham, Isaac, and Jacob"! Later we encounter Joseph and his family, then David and all his family. The focus and purposes of God's activity rest on the generations. It seems that when God calls and touches one man, He is purposing to call and work through his succeeding generations.

I have always been aware of this in my own life and family. I have endeavored to live a godly life in my family and before each member of our family. We have been given 4 sons and 1 daughter. Each of them has married, adding 5 more "adult children" to our family and each one of them is very special to us. From these married children, God has granted to us 14 grandchildren (7 boys and 7 girls). What a challenge and a joy to be the "father" to 26 of us, knowing God has a special purpose for each one of them and that my life is vital to each of them as they come to know God and His purposes for their lives.

God has given us wonderful ways to help encourage one another over the years.

1. **One of my principles was to include our family in our ministry.** Over the years, our children helped with ushering, child care, sound systems operation, choir directing, missions committees,

youth groups, college ministry, and church planting, to mention a few things. This helped them see the value of investing in the kingdom ministry and allowed us to rejoice together when the fruit of our labor began to grow.

2. **We did our best to be together every day around the kitchen table at mealtimes.** This was an invaluable time as we shared our days together and heard what was going on in one another's lives.

3. **We shared our "spiritual markers" with our children** so they knew the times God touched and changed us as a family. One of our children shared with me, "Dad, we don't think that you knew how close we have come to falling away from God. But when the temptations came, we thought of you and Mom and how God has led you and our family, and we just could not do it." I was so glad that I had shared God's work in our family with them.

4. **I constantly shared with our children, "Give God your best! He is God, and deserves nothing less than our best!"** I did not urge them to higher education, but all 5 graduated from both university and seminary. The 4 boys all have earned doctoral degrees from seminaries and all of my children and their spouses continue to serve God and His people.

5. **We have sponsored a family reunion every other year to bring all our children and grandchildren together.** Sometimes we have been able to meet in some pretty amazing places. We also try to gather as a family on special days throughout the year to help them connect with one another and share about what God is doing in their lives.

6. **I have deliberately chosen to write books with each of our 5 children,** introducing them to communicating God's truths through books. God encouraged me to give them the incentive to write on their own long after I am gone.

7. **I have had the privilege of speaking alongside each of our children** in various conference settings, listening carefully as they shared. They have all learned to communicate our "family" message to others in their own unique way, and they do so quite effectively. We are always amazed at what God does through people who put their lives completely into His hands and we are humbled as God continues to give our family members opportunities to write and to proclaim His message around the world.

Our own family has been tremendously important to Marilynn and me, but our church families over the years have been no less important. Serving with God's people has been an absolute thrill over some 50 years of ministry. I have always said God's people are the best people in the world, and God has allowed me the privilege of serving with some of His finest servants.

Tom is my second oldest son. His journey with God has taken him in different directions than my other children. He has served God in several capacities over the years and he and Kim have had unique opportunities to serve the Lord with their family in several countries. They have lived overseas for 7 years, serving God's people in an international church comprised of those in the international business community and the military. Living internationally provides valuable insights into what it means to be family as well as unique challenges in keeping a family strong while living in a foreign language and culture.

In the Scriptures, God uses families. We are so grateful that He is still using ours and we know He will use your family in incredible ways too!

INTRODUCTION

When we began to write this book, Kim and I were slightly reticent. Not because we did not believe in it; we're convinced God uses families all the time in His kingdom. However, we don't want to appear as though we're suggesting our family, the Blackabys, is the example of how families ought to think and act. Certainly God has used my father in significant ways to bless and encourage millions of people through his book *Experiencing God: Knowing and Doing the Will of God*. And yes, each of the members in our family is serving the Lord in various capacities. But this book is about God and what *He* can accomplish through His people. We are keenly aware of how God is using many other families around the world, in amazingly creative capacities.

We do examine the Blackaby family, including many relatives in our extended family who have contributed to our desire to know and to serve God. It's humbling to see how influential and inspirational they've been to us over the years. Though there are examples given from our family background—describing some of the principles the Blackabys have sought to live by—there are many other wonderful families featured in this book, who share stories about their journey with God, to encourage and inspire you.

Walk together with us through the Bible to see the diverse families and how God chose to use them in various ways. God chose some families to raise children He would use later in their lives, God chose other families through whom He would influence many lives, while He invited others to be faithful in simple tasks He had prepared for them to do. Explore the biblical truths and principles in this book and the opportunities to examine your family and your walk with God.

■ You'll find reflective questions and exercises to help you look more closely at how God has designed your family for ministry and service.

- You'll discover ideas to spark your imagination for what God may have in store for you and your children and relatives in serving in His kingdom.
- For small-group study, a Bible study class, or studies with friends, a workbook edition of this book is available called *The Family God Uses: Becoming a Family of Influence* (published by LifeWay Church Resources).

Please understand that this book isn't intended to lay a guilt trip on God's people. It's written in hopes that God will inspire families to see the amazing possibilities for how each family can intentionally be an influence for God in the many different places where He has placed them.

Enjoy this book, prayerfully seeking the heart and mind of God as you read. Listen carefully to what the Holy Spirit may be revealing to you about how He wants to draw your family closer together and how He wants your family to be a light in your neighborhood and world.

Our prayer is that you will continually experience God in your family as you seek and serve Him together and that your family will leave a legacy of faithfulness to God, for generations to follow.

We would like to express our gratitude to the amazing members of North Sea Baptist Church, Stavanger, Norway, for being family to us for seven great years; to the members of First Baptist Church, Biloxi, Mississippi, for their inspiration in all they are doing to help families be families of influence in their community and around the world; and to the thousands of churches and ministries internationally who serve God in the hardest places where the cost to families is so much higher than most people ever know.

■ ■ ■

For we are His workmanship,

created in Christ Jesus for good

works, which God prepared before-

hand that we

should walk in them

(Ephesians 2:10 NKJV).

■ ■ ■

PART 1

GOD'S DESIGN FOR FAMILIES

GOD'S DESIGN AND PURPOSES
FOR THE FAMILY

*O*ne US family has captured attention for decades. Its members have influenced politics, public opinion, international reputations, fashion, lifestyles, and values. Their wealth, celebrity, and power—drawing vast media coverage for more than half a century—have had an impact on society for generations. With one president, several senators, two assassinations, three aircraft crashes, numerous allegations, and one murder conviction, the Kennedy family, for good and for bad, is an example of a single family's legacy of influence.

In every nation, there are influential families. Some very affluent and powerful. Some with companies providing employment to thousands for generations. Certain families have a long line of members involved in politics—or in crime. Others are of royal lineage, or impress the public through their engagement in academics, art, entertainment, medicine, or social reform. These families often pass down their influence, wealth, or power to future generations. Their impact can extend for decades if not centuries. Yet, none leave a more precious legacy than those whom God uses.

The Bible reveals God's creation of the family and His creative work through families throughout history, to leave His mark on humankind. These families carried out His will, obeyed His commands, led faithful lives, and consequently became integral to God's strategy for redeeming lost humanity. These families have not been particularly extraordinary people; most have not been of royal descent, wealthy lineage, and significant power. In fact, we're hard pressed to find that God used any flawless family. Yet one attribute has set apart the families God has used: *their ability to hear God and their willingness to obey Him.* Even through their weaknesses, God has repeatedly shown Himself mighty and trustworthy to do as He has promised through families as they follow Him.

I (Tom) would like to believe I come from a typical middle-class family, but that is probably a bit of a stretch. My family is rooted more so in the bottom fringe of the middle class. On a pastor's salary, feeding and clothing five children meant our family struggled financially as I grew up.

As is with most pastors' families, we were at church whenever the doors were open and our circle of friends was connected to the church in one way or another. In fact, my brother and I married young women who came to Christ through our church and who were part of the youth and student ministries.

I'm not sure there's such a thing as "the model family," but I *am* sure we would not have qualified. We had our struggles, especially with our father being busy most of the time. Yet there was one constant that left a mark on every one of us. This wasn't church per se, or serving together in some capacity, but God Himself. We learned at an early age that when a family honors God in their home, God can do some pretty amazing things through family members.

I look back and shake my head in amazement at some of the results God has been gracious enough to provide through a family with such humble beginnings. Together, without any outside financial support, we've earned 20-plus postsecondary degrees. We've written more than 30 Christian books and resources, including the *Blackaby Study Bible* and several devotional books used around the world. Some of our books have been translated into more than 60 languages and can be found in the homes of everyday people as well as in the offices of leaders of nations. We regularly receive requests to speak at and lead conferences internationally and have been before United Nations delegates, as well as ambassadors, military leaders, and presidents on several occasions.

None of us have sought positions of influence; rather, we've simply accepted whatever invitation God has given us to proclaim His kingdom, wherever this might take us. Any family can become a family that God uses when it makes Him the center of family members' lives and activities and is faithful to do whatever He asks them to do. The Bible is replete with stories about how God chose to work through ordinary families who faithfully followed Him and obeyed what He asked of them.

The family, as God designed it, has increasingly felt society's attacks, special interest groups' criticisms, and the impact of unprecedented moral decline. Christians should not forget that whatever God created for good, Satan has sought to destroy. This is no different for the family. From the beginning, at God's creation, the family was there, and right beside the family was evil. In the Genesis creation account, at the end of each day, God looked at what He had created and saw that it was "good."

- Genesis 1:4: "And God saw the light that it was good." (NKJV)
- Genesis 1:10: "And God called the dry land Earth, and the gathering together of the waters He called Seas. And God saw that it was good." (NKJV)
- Genesis 1:12: After God created the plant world, "God saw that it was good." (NKJV)
- Genesis 1:31: "And God saw everything that he had made, and indeed it was very good." (NKJV)

The Bible then records in Genesis 2:18 that while God was talking with Adam, He stated there was a problem. Every creature had companions—other creatures of its kind to interact with—except Adam. "And the Lord God said [for the first time], it is *not good* that man should be alone; I will make for him a helper comparable to him" (NKJV; author emphasis added). From that time forward, God established the family. It is important to understand that humankind was not created simply to procreate and subdue the earth as some think.

- Consider the difference between humankind and the rest of creation. Some animals bond for life or group together in some hierarchical fashion for protection and community, but no other creatures besides humankind have lifelong bonds characterized by deep sacrificial relationships. We were created to have relationships of permanency, with God and with one another, to set us apart from every other creature on earth. And God had specific purposes in mind when He ordained the family.

Companionship

According to Genesis 2:18, God looked at Adam and saw he had a need other creatures could not address. So God created Eve, and together Adam and Eve became inseparable, for good and for bad! They walked with God together. Then they sinned against God together, were cast out of the Garden of Eden together, and they had children together—but at least they were together! Companionship is a primary aspect of family that should never be underestimated. We were never meant to be alone. We need each other and God understands this. That's why He promises to "[set] the lonely in families" (Psalm 68:6 NIV) and that, as His children, we can be assured of His constant presence. Jesus said, "I will never leave you nor forsake you" (Hebrews 13:5 NKJV). That is why He holds those lacking family close to His heart and is the protector of widows and orphans (Exodus 22:22–23).

Within the family we communicate, share in what God is doing, and support each other. Mel Blackaby offers this example, "I try to take each of our children out from time to time and share with them what I see God doing. I also ask them what they feel God is doing in their lives and how I can pray for them."

In my immediate family, our Christmas tradition includes sitting down with hot cider in hand and a plate of sweet and savory snacks and each person recounting his or her year and how God has answered prayers. And when we chose to accept our current ministry position, we needed to move back to Canada from Norway. We sat down together as a family and processed what God was doing in our lives as we moved toward that decision. We talked about how God had been working in our hearts, giving us a sense that He was preparing to change the focus in our lives, and then asked our children what they were sensing God telling them. Together as a family we chose to accept the new adventure God placed before us. This togetherness is significant to us and to God.

Noah persevered many years in a lonely task. I doubt he could have accomplished it without his family at his side. Our families can support and encourage us in our obedience to God even if others misunderstand. This form of companionship is important in God's plan for His people.

In fact, one primary role the Holy Spirit fulfills in God's family is companionship. The Greek word to describe the Spirit is *parakletos*, meaning "comforter, companion, counselor, or advocate"; Christ promised that He would never leave us (John 14:16; Hebrews 13:5)!

Training

Families are God's training ground for life, where children learn the fundamentals for building strong relationships.

- Love
- Trust and respect for others
- Sharing
- Honoring one another
- Obeying authority
- Working together
- Sacrifice
- Carrying out responsibilities
- Integrity
- Honesty
- Grace and forgiveness
- Hard work
- Prayer
- Commitment
- Christian values

So much more is learned in the family. When people *don't* learn relationship fundamentals in the family, they struggle. Sadly, prisons are full of people who failed to learn these fundamentals at home. Communities pay a heavy price when the family role has disintegrated. Individuals without a godly upbringing suffer in worse ways.

Often children come to view God in much the same way as they view their fathers. If a girl's father is a strict disciplinarian, she may view God as harsh and judgmental. If a boy's dad is kind, forgiving, and generous, he can view God as compassionate, caring, and nurturing. Many Christians correlate their relationship with their heavenly Father and their relationship with their earthly father.

God wants godly parents to help children have a proper, healthy view of who He is. Yet, many children today grow up actually running from the God their parents serve because of how dysfunctional their home life is! Others come to know and love God at an early age because their home is filled with loving parents who offer grace, compassion, trust, and a quiet strength that cause the children to draw near to God. When God has access to the parents' hearts, the home becomes a wonderful place where He is honored and where children—and their friends—are drawn into His presence.

Protection

Families innately desire to protect one another. Humans keep their young with them longer than any other creature. Their babies take decades to grow to the point of being able to survive independently. Other creatures separate from their young right after birth or several months later. Yet some humans are trying to oust offspring after 30 years! Many others continue—well after their children have left home—to do their laundry, help them financially, and raise grandchildren.

Protect. Every child knows that's what big brothers or big sisters do! Parents "go to bat" for their children in many areas of life because of a deep bond. Later, the tables turn as children begin to care for aging parents unable to care for themselves, by taking their parents into their homes or finding suitable accommodations for them.

Family members try to protect one another against making unwise choices; those who would harm, abuse, or cheat them; and providing medical attention to thwart illness. The phrase "Blood is thicker than water" recognizes the family bond and the mutual sacrifices family members are willing to make throughout life together.

My father remembers vividly an incident at a high school soccer game. Three of his sons were playing on the team together when an opposing player unnecessarily and roughly tackled the youngest of the three. Within minutes, the two older, stronger brothers introduced that player to a strong (and legal) message of caution, should he consider hurting their little brother in the future.

Community Foundation

It's in the family that we learn to become productive members of society. In places where communities have a strong sense of responsibility toward one another, where people care for one another's children and respect one another's property, they have a real sense of "we" and "ours" rather than "me" and "mine." In these communities, streets are cleaner; children safer; and playgrounds, picnic areas, and recreation centers are well used.

Crime rates are lower where strong family values prevail. Vandalism is lower when good community programs and sports clubs support families. Property theft is drastically reduced where there is a strong sense of community. Bicycles are brought to their rightful homes, wallets and purses are returned to their owners untouched, and people watch out for one another when family values are taught and practiced.

Representative of the Kingdom of God

The earthly family is a picture of God's eternal family. It's fascinating to see how God alluded to family when describing Himself, His kingdom, and His people. For example,

- "My house shall be called a house of prayer" (Matthew 21:13 NKJV).
- "Our Father which art in heaven" (Matthew 6:9 KJV).
- "But as many as received Him, to them He gave the right to become children of God, to those who believe in His name" (John 1:12 NKJV).
- "The Spirit Himself bears witness with our spirit that we are children of God, and if children, then heirs—heirs of God and joint heirs with Christ" (Romans 8:16–17 NKJV).

- "In My Father's house are many mansions; if it were not so, I would have told you. I go to prepare a place for you" (John 14:2 NKJV).
- "For whoever does the will of My Father in heaven is My brother and sister and mother" (Matthew 12:50 NKJV).
- "For this reason I bow my knees to the Father of our Lord Jesus Christ, from whom the whole family in heaven and earth is named" (Ephesians 3:14–15 NKJV).

When Christ's disciples asked Him to teach them to pray, Jesus could have taught them to address God in many different ways: God of Heaven and Earth, Almighty Creator, Holy One of Israel, or used any of the Old Testament names of God such as Banner, Healer, Provider, and Lord God. Instead, He chose to have them approach God with the intimate term: Father.

Jesus had introduced God as Heavenly Father in His Sermon on the Mount (Matthew 5:16, 45, 48; 6:1, 4), but we don't know if Christ's disciples had previously considered addressing Almighty Creator, All-Powerful God as Father. When Jesus taught His disciples to pray, He was doing more than modeling a spiritual discipline; He was helping His followers understand the kind of relationship God wants to have with His people.

We're hard-pressed to find any other religion that offers such an intimate relationship with God—a Creator who is above and beyond all human comprehension, yet who desires to relate to people as a healthy human father relates to his children. It's noteworthy that the Greek word normally translated *father* also includes the nuances of a male ancestor, parent, and guardian. On many occasions God demonstrated the care of a parent toward His people and of a guardian protecting them from their enemies.

Building Block of the Church

The family helps us envision how the local church is to function. Just as God intended for every child to be born into a family, so every new believer is born into the kingdom of God, and a local church, a faith community. The church is to be family to fellow believers and to nurture and care for them as family members care for one another. In the church new believers grow and mature. Everyone learns about the fundamentals of faith and belief in God, and each one contributes by using his or her gifts and abilities for the betterment of all. We'll explore this more in later chapters, but it's evident that where there are strong families, there is also a strong church. And where there is a strong church, families are also strengthened and equipped to participate together in God's kingdom.

We know of churches comprised of students, churches in prisons, churches in nursing homes, churches on military bases, even churches on TV! However, a church in the fullest sense will look like a family. There will be white-haired people, babies, and Christians of every age in between, married people, single people, blue-, brown-, and green-eyed people, new Christians, and old Christians. Going to church should be like a family reunion every week!

Yet many Christians seem to have forgotten that God has expectations for His people. They come to God as they are but on their own terms. Throughout the Bible, *God* has set the requirements for what is acceptable in His presence. God rejects that which is offered to Him in worship and sacrifice when it does not meet His standards and requirements. Likewise, God has expectations for His people regarding their home lives.

Proverbs 22:6 (ASV) affirms this principle, "Train up a child in the way he should go, and even when he is old he will not depart from it." Some people have taken this to be a *promise* from God when, it is actually a *principle* to follow. This verse is not providing a guarantee but a principle, a guideline for parents to follow as they raise their children. It may be that a son or daughter will depart from the Lord for a time, but the teachings will never depart from them!

How often do we discuss spiritual things with our children or with our spouse? How much do we depend on Sunday School teachers, youth leaders, or pastors to teach our family about God rather than doing so ourselves?

"It was my parents' steadfast and complete trust in Christ tl influenced me as a child," writes Carrie Blackaby Webb. "They confronted many challenges through the years and each was met with the confidence that God would help them through—and He did. The same God who was so faithful to my parents is the same God who is now faithful to me and my family as we serve on the missions field. The absolute confidence of God's presence and that our lives are in His hands has carried us through many trials, and it is my hope that our children both see and experience what it means to fully trust in the Lord and His faithfulness."

The Old Testament period was God's training ground for His people and an opportunity for them to develop godly habits in their worship of Him and in their relationships with people. But they chose repeatedly, at home, in businesses, and in worship, to follow other priorities, worldly values and secular morals, and to abandon God's ways. This was exactly what God tried to protect His people from; He knew what the consequences would be for their families and their communities—far different from the purposes and design we find in His Word. □

GOD'S DESIGN FOR FAMILY LIFE

*G*od is well aware of the importance of family life, and from Scripture we can see that He provides importance safeguards to protect the family. The Bible reveals the roots of the Jewish family model and its longstanding traditions of loyalty to relatives, responsibility toward both children and parents, passing on blessings to children, and living life so that a person's reputation and character would allow peaceful coexistence with neighbors.

Where a person's family came from and who he or she was related to could mean life or death in some situations. It also opened doors to opportunity and influence in others. Family lines have always been important to God's people, so much so that Christ's lineage is given in Matthew and Luke to demonstrate to readers His legitimacy as the Messiah.

When God brought the children of Israel out from Egyptian slavery, He gave them guidelines to use to develop their new society. His laws and commandments were to teach them how to treat one another and live in harmony. The Books of Leviticus and Deuteronomy are essentially their manuals to help the people love the Lord their God with all their heart, soul, strength, and mind and to love their neighbor as themselves.

Three of His Ten Commandments pertain specifically to families. The fifth commandment requires children to honor their father and mother and ensures the ongoing viability of the family institution (Deuteronomy 5:16; Exodus 20:12). It is in the dishonoring of parents that society begins to break down and civil strife grows. Both father and mother were to be honored equally, not in some hierarchical fashion or one at the expense of the other. They may have different roles in the home, but the children are to honor them both, and both should honor each other (1 Peter 2:17; 3:7).

The seventh commandment (Exodus 20:14; Deuteronomy 5:18) preserves the family from immoral activity and destructive behaviors by the parents. It provides security in the home and enshrines a model of respect and honor for one's spouse. By commanding that all sexual relations be kept in the home, the design is for every child to be born into a family with parents. Society today is reeling from the epidemic disregard for this commandment.

Children are being born without a father in the home, men neglect their responsibility for the children they've fathered, and women live with the consequences of promiscuity, fornication, and adultery without the support of a father and a husband at home. Due largely to the disregard of this commandment, society is paying a heavy price with overflowing prisons, ever-expanding welfare systems, disadvantaged children, and rampant crime.

The tenth commandment also directly pertains to family life. God lists as examples what is not to be coveted; that which is essential to family life: the wife, the house, the property and the animals (Deuteronomy 5:21; Exodus 20:17). If any of these specifics were removed, it would be extremely detrimental to the family. It is clear that, in the Ten Commandments, God's intent was to provide a hedge of protection around the family for its survival and to help the family thrive for the benefit of society as a whole.

Jesus Upheld the Design

In His teachings, Jesus affirmed His Father's desire to protect the family, particularly as He offered expanded versions of Old Testament teachings. Though He never married, Jesus held high regard for the value of a man and woman coming together as one in marriage. In one particular exchange, Jesus affirms marriage and discourages divorce.

> The Pharisees came and asked Him, "Is it lawful for a man to divorce his wife?" testing Him. And He answered and said to them, "What did Moses command you?" They said, "Moses permitted a man to write a certificate of divorce, and to dismiss her." And Jesus answered and said to them, "Because of the hardness of your heart he wrote you this precept. But from the beginning of the creation, God 'made them male and female.' 'For this reason a man shall leave his father and mother and be joined to his wife, and the two shall become one flesh'; so then they are no longer two, but one flesh. Therefore what God has joined together, let not man separate." In the house His disciples also asked Him again about the same matter. So He said to them, "Whoever divorces his wife and marries another commits adultery against her. And if a woman divorces her husband and marries another, she commits adultery" (Mark 10:2–12 NKJV).

Christ's teachings appear to some as rather strict in light of today's record number of broken marriages, but He was well aware of divorce's consequences in the husband's and wife's, the children's, and the extended family's lives. It's no secret that both divorce and adultery (people call it "having an affair") leave deep wounds and can scar people for the rest of their lives. Not only did God want His people to avoid that pain, but also God knew the negative fallout would continue for generations—just as the positive influence of a godly marriage leaves its mark on future generations. Barton Priebe's story is one illustration of the latter.

Barton shepherds a church in a megacity and, by all accounts, is a great preacher; a well-organized, godly man; and passionate about helping God's people live their Christianity authentically. He strongly believes in fathers leading their wife and children in family worship times and encourages his church members to do so. This is his heritage.

Barton's father also was a faithful pastor who served churches for three decades before becoming a chaplain in a seniors' housing complex. His grandfather was a construction worker and lay pastor who preached Bible truths in small churches every Sunday night. His great-grandfather was an itinerant evangelist who canvassed Canadian prairie provinces, preaching the gospel all of his adult life. That's not all. His brother is a missionary to an unreached tribe in Tanzania. His uncle and aunt, Del and Joyce, were missionaries in Kenya for 20 years, and Del now serves as a pastor in Canada. Del's aunt gave her life to missions in Africa.

Barton can't remember a time when his parents ever pressured any of their three children to go into the ministry. In fact, they were more likely to discourage this because of the well-known challenges and hardships many pastors' families often endure. Yet their passion for Christ and love for God's people were so contagious that all three children serve the Lord—and married women who love the Lord and together support churches. What is the strategy for a family maintaining a proper focus on relationship with Him? God provides the key in Deuteronomy 6:1–9, 12–13 (NKJV):

"Now this is the commandment, and these are the statutes and judgments which the Lord your God has commanded to teach you, that you may observe them in the land which you are crossing over to possess, that you may fear the Lord your God, to keep all His statutes and His commandments which I command you, you and your son and your grandson, all the days of your life, and that your days may be prolonged. Therefore hear, O Israel, and be careful to observe it, that it may be well with you, and that you may multiply greatly as the Lord God of your fathers has promised you—'a land flowing with milk and honey.'

"Hear, O Israel: The Lord our God, the Lord is one! You shall love the Lord your God with all your heart, with all your soul, and with all your strength.

"And these words which I command you today shall be in your heart. You shall teach them diligently to your children, and shall talk of them when you sit in your house, when you walk by the way, when you lie down, and when you rise up. You shall bind them as a sign on your hand, and they shall be as frontlets between your eyes. You shall write them on the doorposts of your house and on your gates....

"Then beware, lest you forget the Lord who brought you out of the land of Egypt, from the house of bondage. You shall fear the Lord your God and serve Him, and shall take oaths in His name."

God expects every family to place Him at the very center of their home. His desire is that all parents would

- spend regular time with their children, sharing truths about Him;
- instruct children in the ways of God, in relation to others around them;
- teach children how God desires to be a part of every aspect of their lives;

- maintain the influence of a relationship with God through the generations.

In Deuteronomy 6, God has outlined His strategy for His people to maintain their relationship with Him. This was to have a generational impact and allow them to experience all that He planned for them. The key to this was and is the family.

- **A love relationship with God is to be lived and demonstrated. (v. 5)**

A relationship with God will naturally work itself out in our daily actions before our children. There are hundreds of ways we demonstrate our relationship with God, including seeking time with Him, worshipping Him, and following His commands. We demonstrate our love for Him in remaining faithful through the years, never denying Him, and trusting Him to be faithful to do what He has promised. When our children watch our lives, there should be no doubt that we love God.

- **God's Word would be known by heart. (v. 6)**

Psalm 119:11 speaks of hiding God's Word in our heart so that we will not sin against God. Knowing His Word means more than repetition. It means allowing it to wash over our lives and become a part of who we are. We must ask ourselves, "Do I desire to know God's commands and truths by heart? In what practical ways am I endeavoring to be familiar with God's Word and His ways personally?"

- **God's Word would be taught (v. 7)**

Carefully (diligently, pointedly, intensively, purposefully) taught. It takes deliberate effort to purposefully teach God's truths to our children. Bible stories, family devotions, Sunday School, and Bible studies are some ways to do this—to have God direct everything we do impresses on children that God has first place.

- **God's Word would be applied (v. 7)**

God's expectation is that parents will consult Him and His Word in everyday situations as they arise. As mothers and fathers, we should look to include spiritual conversations in everyday life as we walk along the road, as we greet our children in the morning, as we put them to bed at night, even putting reminders all around our homes. This shows great respect and regard for the Word of God as being trustworthy and the foundation upon which a family can be built.

▪ God's Word would be visible (v. 8)

Framing Scripture on the walls of your home, above the doors, stitched into pillows, and elsewhere is an everyday reminder of what's important in your home and to your family. This serves as a reminder to whom the family belongs: God is central to its identity. Identity is important to children—where they come from, what their heritage is, who their relatives are—because it helps them know that they belong. Belonging creates a sense of values, teaches acceptable behaviors, and gives purpose and meaning to people. Probably the most important aspect of this is to help children know the Bible from an early age. If you were to walk into your house, what would you notice first? What prominence does God's Word have in your home?

▪ God's deeds would be remembered (v. 12)

Remembering God's deeds gives us a sense of history with God. We can spend time regularly reviewing how God has helped our family through difficult times or how He has blessed us in various ways. Writing down some of the family experiences or creating physical reminders of each time God answered a prayer will also build a strong foundation of faith in the family. In the Old Testament, God's people set up piles of stones that served as markers of special times when God intervened in their lives. Families today can write reminders on stones and place these in their gardens as visible reminders of God's goodness.

▪ Reverence, obedience, and service to God would be demonstrated (vv. 1–2, 13)

Think about the last time you worshipped together as a family. Did you sit together as a family? It's important for our children to see us singing the songs, putting money in the offering plate, and opening our own Bible to read along in the Scripture passage. Each of these actions is a teaching tool that communicates to children reverence for God. We must not use His name in vain or in an empty fashion. Following God's commands even when we do not feel like it and going out of our way to help others in need indicate to our children how important our relationship with God is.

Walking It Out

I (Tom) call Deuteronomy 6:6–9 my "kicking-rock" passage. We live a good 15-minute walk from my youngest son's elementary school. We have to go down the back alley, cross over to a pathway that snakes beside a forest, across a footbridge over a creek, up a short hill through a neighborhood, and on to the school. There are lots of bugs and slugs to avoid on the pathway, but the walk is pleasant and pretty. On one of the first days of walking to school we happened upon a perfect kicking rock. Just round and flat enough to skip a good distance if you kicked it just right.

Conor and I take turns kicking the rock as we go, trying to get it to go as far as possible. The challenge is to keep it from dropping off the bridge into the water, falling down a drainage grate, getting stuck under a car, or lost in the tall grass along the pathway. But as we go, I ask about what his day holds for him (*kick*). We talk about how to handle bullies at school (*kick*). We look at God's creation along the pathway, the flowers and the various creatures (*kick*). We talk about how to be a good influence on his friends at school (kick), and we pray about the challenges he may be having at the time (*kick*). Occasionally we challenge each other to remember Bible verses or stories (*kick*).

All the while, I'm instilling godly values, good morals, a sense of identity (who he belongs to), and looking at what he is to become with God's help. Our kicking-rock time is special to me because it is a time when I can share with my son what is on my heart for him, and how God is such an important part of our home, family, and individual lives.

Jack McGorman, a seminary professor of New Testament studies, once told the story of walking his granddaughter to preschool. He described her pretty dress and her golden hair, her winning smile and bright personality, and then noted her legs were of normal length for a small child, but quite short in comparison to his own. He stated he had a right to walk as fast as he wanted to walk. That he could even choose to run if he wanted, but doing so would hurt his young granddaughter. He chose instead to take smaller steps. Because of his love for this child, he walked at a comfortable pace for her.

He compares this to the Christian life as we walk with younger Christians. As mature Christians, we have a right to charge on ahead discussing and debating the deeper truths of the kingdom of God. But out of respect for the younger Christians in the faith, we choose to take smaller steps, to walk more slowly through the Scriptures so they can keep up and grow at a pace suitable to their ability and understanding.

> TEACHABLE MOMENTS ARE GREAT FOR THIS, TAKING ORDINARY OPPORTUNITIES ALONG THE WAY TO EXPLAIN GOD AND THE CHRISTIAN LIFE TO OUR CHILDREN IN AN INTENTIONAL WAY, A WAY THAT ALSO WILL INFLUENCE FUTURE GENERATIONS.

I've seen many parents over the years who charge full throttle through supermarkets or down sidewalks, dragging their small children at an alarming pace despite their cries and protests. I've genuinely been afraid for these children, thinking any moment an arm is going to be pulled out of the socket! I've also seen parents who demand that their children sit perfectly still through deep, long, and boring sermons, expecting them to learn something spiritual. These children are the ones who later may vow to never step foot in a church again when they have a choice.

The better option, of course, is to walk at a child's pace and to help a child to learn spiritual things at a child's level. The teachable moments are great for this, taking ordinary opportunities along the way to explain God and the Christian life to our children in an intentional way, a way that also will influence future generations. ☐

BEING A FAMILY OF INFLUENCE—
GOD'S STRATEGY
AND OUR OBEDIENCE

*J*esus said,

> You are the light of the world. A city that is set on a hill can-
> not be hidden. Nor do they light a lamp and put it under a
> basket, but on a lampstand, and it gives light to all who are
> in the house. Let your light so shine before men, that they
> may see your good works and glorify your Father in heaven
> (Matthew 5:14–16 NKJV).

It's easy to hide among the other families at the school or become
like all the other families in the neighborhood and not stand out,
not make waves, not challenge the status quo, and not be the one
to take the initiative. When Jesus said these words in Matthew 5,
He was not providing us an option to be light; He was declaring
that when we commit our lives to Him, we *are* light as He is light.
The choice comes in whether or not we will hide our light or let
our light shine brightly. Letting your light shine as a family can be
both fun and challenging as you let God work through you and as
you experience His faithfulness in the midst of trying times.

Many of the well-known biblical figures, such as Abraham,
Jacob, Moses, Jethro, and the young David lived nomadic lives
herding their flocks about the countryside making a living off
the land. They were hardworking people growing their own food,
making their own clothing, or trading for goods in the market
places. What was noticeable about many of the families that worshipped God was their conspicuous ability to influence people
around them.

- Wherever Abraham went, people noticed. God had blessed him to the point that he was a formidable and wealthy businessman (Genesis 23:6).
- Jacob's son Joseph became the second most powerful man in Egypt, saving the lives of thousands through God's gift of wisdom and dream interpretation.
- Though educated in Egypt, Moses cut his teeth guiding flocks in the Sinai wilderness, the same place he later would guide God's people and defeat the armies of the surrounding nations. Everywhere Moses led the people, they had an impact on cities, towns, villages, and numerous tribes.

Through Noah, his wife, and their three married sons, God decided to "start over again" with a new family, one that would be faithful to Him (Genesis 6–9 NKJV). "By faith Noah, . . . moved with godly fear, prepared an ark for the saving of his household, by which he condemned the world and became heir of the righteousness which is according to faith" (Hebrews 11:7 NKJV). This was more than simply a practical measure ensuring that the earth would be repopulated through four married couples. Noah was chosen not for his ability to bear children, but for his faithfulness and willingness to serve God.

When God called Abram, his whole family became a part of the new covenant (Genesis 12:2–3). Together they were all uprooted from friends and relatives and homeland, and they followed God—as a family. Abraham (as he would later be called), his wife, Sarai, and their promised son, Isaac, would eventually found the human lineage through which Christ would be born and bring salvation to the world.

In fact, throughout the Bible, God is referred to quite often as the God of Abraham, Isaac, and Jacob (Isaac's second-born son), reminding generation after generation that God uses families in very significant ways. This has brought hope to many people who knew that if God used multiple generations of families in the past, He could do so again in the future. His past actions connect with His future promises.

It's a fascinating exercise to look back in one's family history and imagine what it was like for people in previous generations. Those forbears living in a vastly different cultural context or faraway country. What went through these ancestors' minds when they decided—or were challenged—to immigrate to new lands? What were their fears and hopes? Did they envision a brighter future for their generations?

The Blackaby family tree contains a wide variety of individuals of every occupation and station in life. There are teachers, preachers, entrepreneurs, soldiers, pilots, bankers, missionaries, homemakers, authors, basketball referees, high school counselors—the list seems endless. But generation after generation is marked with God's guiding hand on those who responded to His love. From those whom Charles Spurgeon sponsored to attend his pastor's college in England, to those who fought in the Great War (World War I) and survived, to those who left home and family to start a new life in far-off countries, God has been vigilant in His care, protection, and guidance. God had in mind to accomplish something in the Blackabys' future. When you look at your extended family and relatives, can you identify a line of faithfulness or are you more like Noah, whom God used to start a line of faithfulness?

My grandfather, G. R. S. Blackaby, fought in World War I as part of the Canadian forces and knew without any doubt that God protected him. His third son, my uncle William Blackaby, relates that on one occasion. G. R. S. was posted as a night sentry and needed to take a walk out behind a small hill. Suddenly the enemy began a barrage of shelling. He finished quickly and headed back toward where he had been posted. A fellow soldier saw him and turned ghostly white. He said, "Is that you, Blackie?"

Granddad said, "Yes."

The fellow insisted, "Let me touch you to make sure!" After touching him, he walked with Granddad to where he had been standing behind the small hill and showed him a crater 12 feet across. There was no question about Granddad's conviction and character. He knew that his life was in God's hands and he never worried. This was the man who would become the father of three sons, the middle son being Henry. This was the man who would shape and influence my father, Henry T. Blackaby, after whom I'm named.

All throughout the history of God's people, God has looked for families through whom He could lead His people or bless them, or bring them back into relationship with Him when they strayed.

- When His people needed a leader through whom God would free them from Egyptian slavery, He turned to Amram and Jochebed and their three children Miriam, Aaron, and little brother Moses (Exodus 6:16–20).
- When God sought to establish a people through whom He could reveal Himself to a world and bless all mankind, He appointed an older couple named Abram and Sarai and the son they would later bear, Isaac (Genesis 12:1).
- When God decided on a judge to guide and protect His people who were being oppressed, He turned to the family of Manoah to whom a son named Samson would be born (Judges 13).
- When God sought a king to rule over His people—one who would worship Him and faithfully lead His people—He turned to the family of Jesse and through Samuel chose a shepherd boy named David.
- When He ordained a home to nurture His own Son, God turned to a young couple named Mary and Joseph who would care for and love Jesus as their own.

Miriam, Aaron, Isaac, Samson, David, and Jesus grew up in homes that honored the Lord and who sought after God for wisdom and guidance. They grew up in homes where God was an important part of their daily lives. If God were to look for a family to work powerfully through today, if God were looking for a family He could trust with a difficult assignment, would yours be one of those He could choose? As parents are faithful to follow God, it creates the opportunity for their children to have the same blessings and relationship with God as they had. Consider Abraham's influence on Isaac.

Abraham: A Godly Father

As long as Abraham was faithful to the covenant relationship God made with him, it created the opportunity for Isaac to enjoy the same kind of covenant relationship with God that Abraham enjoyed. The covenant was renewed with Isaac; and as he was faithful, Jacob, his son, was given the chance to have the same kind of covenant relationship with God. The biblical narrative shows that:

- Abraham obeyed God the moment God spoke and called him out of his home country to follow Him (Genesis 12:1).
- Abraham and Sarah stepped out in faith, left all their comforts of civilized life and became nomads trusting that the God who called them would be true to His word.
- Abraham had to persevere through tough times, military conflict, enemy raids, several international relocations, yet remained faithful.
- Abraham honored God, grew in his relationship and understanding of God, took a stand for God, listened to God, prayed to Him and sought God throughout his life, and consequently was tremendously blessed by God.

This was the home in which Isaac grew up. How do we know about Abraham's faith journey with God before Isaac was born? Because he told these stories to Isaac and they were passed down to succeeding generations and recorded. Abraham was the dad who modeled for his son what a devoted life looked like. Abraham was not just a *religious* person. He didn't worship God or pray for show simply to improve his reputation in the community. He didn't say *one* thing in the presence of God and then go and do *another* before his family. Isaac saw his dad's commitment to follow God when his father tied him up, put him on the altar, and tearfully raised a knife to sacrifice his only son in obedience to

God's command! Surely *that* would have left an indelible mark on young Isaac, who learned that day who was the most important person in his father's life.

Isaac saw God test his dad's faithfulness and he saw his dad pass the test. We may wonder if that test was as much for Isaac to see as it was for Abraham to pass! God had a great assignment for Abraham, and He wanted to know if he was up to the challenge. And God also had specific assignments for Isaac and Isaac's son, grandson, and great-grandson. Father Abraham's faithfulness not only left an impression on Isaac, but has influenced every person who has read this history, to this day.

God's Strategy for Influence

God's primary strategy has always been to use His people to be agents of change. This strategy was deployed not just in Bible stories—it continues all around us today! Barton Priebe found two consistent responses from the pastors' kids he questioned, who had stopped pursuing a relationship with God and abandoned the church. Either they saw their pastor father as a hypocrite who did not live out in the home the principles he preached in the pulpit, or they felt their father loved the church more than his children. Yet other pastors' kids never built up resentment towards God and the church, because their father maintained a good balance between family time and ministry time.

These kids saw their parents' Christianity as authentic and genuine. They not only pursued a relationship with God and continued in church, but also developed a deep love for the church and God's people and shared in their parents' ministry. God uses families to influence their communities, offices, companies, schools, organizations, and neighborhoods.

Esther influenced the Assyrian king, an entire nation, and its decrees, and the Jewish people. Joseph saved a nation from starvation by implementing seven years of conservation strategies in Egypt. Daniel's influence in Babylon was far-reaching during his lifetime. Recent history demonstrates how Christian world leaders have helped to avert wars, quell conflict between nations, and offer justice where the rule of law has been abandoned. Some of the most powerful nations the world has ever seen have been led by men and women who come before the Lord God Almighty on bended knee.

God's people have always been people of influence because they serve a mighty God and a living Lord. There is no question that the Christian values and Christian people has significantly influenced the Western world. Kings, queens, presidents, and prime ministers alike have prayed to God, studied His Word, asking Him to guide their decisions as they lead their countries.

What God does at a national level through His people is as significant to Him as what He does at a personal level, even as one family prays for neighbors to come to Christ. There's no limit to what God can do through His people when they are available to Him and willing to obey.

Time and again we see how
- God can use one or two faithful families to affect entire towns, villages, and communities;
- one godly business owner can motivate a multinational corporation;
- godly teachers are changing lives for eternity as they faithfully bear witness to the activity of God in their own lives;
- godly military leaders, prison guards, doctors, clerks, law enforcement personnel, coaches, lawyers, and thousands more are allowing God to use them to change lives and communities all around them.

Two contemporary illustrations come to mind. The first family sensed God calling them to reach people in "closed" countries or countries currently antagonistic to Christians. Of a different nationality, this family wouldn't be subjected to suspicions or snubs Americans would face normally. In fact, they faced few restrictions in Muslim countries and would be able to enter such countries "under the radar." They brainstormed and, following the example of the Apostle Paul, a tent-maker by trade, they developed a company to provide services the closed countries needed. Although God richly blessed their company's material success, the family's joy came from being able to share God's love with people who had no other opportunity to experience it and being able to live a life of faithfulness to God before people.

Another family, the Schroeders, decided to spend their summer vacation reaching out to poor, disadvantaged people in Mexico after hearing from a friend about a church planter who organizes missions trips. The parents and their three kids determined to roll up their sleeves and serve in any way they could. They prepared skits from Youth with a Mission (YWAM resources). Ev, the mom, choreographed a dance to a Spanish worship song. Week one, they served with local churches scattered across the remote areas of the northern Baja. They camped on the US side of the border, and each morning travelled across the border to connect with a village church and bring the gospel message in engaging ways for children and adults (bubbles, skits, dance, and preaching). Of course, they had to visit Disneyland for a few days on the way home!

These and many other families have understood the challenge and have sought to do what they can for God's kingdom. Yet other Christian families do not yet grasp the significance of God's call on their lives. They seem to exist with little understanding of their role in the kingdom of God and minimal, if any, effort to reach others and help them experience Him, and the peace, joy, blessings, guidance, and purpose He alone provides. We pray every Christian family, including yours, will continually seek through spiritual eyes opportunities to be involved in His kingdom work. This work is all around us, and God has designed specific work for each family to do in obedience to Him.

Obedience and Influence

God has chosen to use families, their children, and their succeeding generations in various ways, as long as they remained faithful to Him. In Exodus 29, God gives instructions relating to the role of the High Priest, and to those chosen by God to serve in this position, including Moses's older brother, Aaron. But included in these instructions were directives to the sons who would follow in Aaron's footsteps. The role of the High Priest was incredibly important to the people of Israel; their lives depended on him performing this office before God and on behalf of the people. It's interesting to see how God chose to work through Aaron's family as a priestly order. Everything about them was to be dedicated to the Lord and their whole lives were to be given to studying for and performing the acts of priests to the Lord God. The Bible provides the specifics.

"Take the other ram—the ram used for dedication—and tell Aaron and his sons to put their hands on its head. Kill it, and take some of its blood and put it on the lobes of the right ears of Aaron and his sons, on the thumbs of their right hands and on the big toes of their right feet. Throw the rest of the blood against all four sides of the altar. Take some of the blood that is on the altar and some of the anointing oil, and sprinkle it on Aaron and his clothes and on his sons and their clothes. He, his sons, and their clothes will then be dedicated to me.... Aaron's priestly garments are to be handed on to his sons after his death, for them to wear when they are ordained. The son of Aaron who succeeds him as priest and who goes into the Tent of my presence to serve in the Holy Place is to wear these garments for seven days" (Exodus 29:19–21, 29–30 GNT).

Had Aaron ever decided to abandon God and his role as High Priest, God likely would have chosen another family through which He would speak to His people. How Aaron walked before the Lord determined the livelihood and ministry of the generations that followed him. The same is true for us.

D. K. Hale writes about his family who left Texas to homestead in northern Alberta, Canada, in the mid-50s. "In the summer of 1958, Mom and a young guy were trying to get a message to Dad, who was down on the flats of the Peace River, where he had a sheep camp. After riding several hours on a horse and winding her way down the long rolling hills to the river cabin, in the darkness she lost her way. Seeing the small kerosene lamp shining in the window of the cabin, she called out to Dad in the dark of the night. The man working for Dad heard Mom, came outside, and hollered back to Mom telling her to wait and he would come and get her.

The next morning, the hired man took mom and showed why he had stopped her the night before. Only a very short distance ahead of where she had headed was a sharp drop-off. Mom said she believed the Lord spoke to her heart immediately and said, 'Louise, I brought you and Keith (Dad) to a place where you were to provide spiritual light and you have been trying to put out that light by crying and wanting to go back to Texas.' He then told her, 'I am tired of your complaining about how hard it is, and I want it stopped.' She was an absolutely changed woman and was a phenomenal wife and ministry partner to my father until death parted them in January 2002. Two of her sons became pastors in Canada, one worked for a national convention of churches, and the others continue to serve as faithful Christian ranchers and businessmen in their community." The legacy and impact of the Hale family continues to this day.

Each of us should consider the impact our response to God will have not only on us individually but also on our families, our children and their futures, and our future generations. God is able to graciously bless our children, in spite of parents. However, I wonder if there ever was a time I refused God's direction that removed God's intended blessings for my children.

Many of the families God uses do not come into His service until they are adequately prepared by God ahead of time. There seems to be a time of equipping and training, a time of testing and shaping that God allows before He invites families into larger responsibilities. What we do for God is not what we can manufacture, but that which God reveals to us when we are ready. Then we respond to His invitations and watch Him accomplish what He intends to through us. □

FAMILY-TIME
REFLECTIONS

1. If you haven't already done so, will you commit to making God the obvious priority in your home?

2. Will you commit to having your "kicking-rock" time with each of your children? What might that look like?

3. Will you commit to living an authentic, genuine Christian life for the sake of your children who desperately need a godly heritage?

4. Are you in the place today where you would hear God nudging you if He were to call your family into service?

5. Would you be willing, without hesitation, to step out in faith even if the road were hard and the way difficult?

6. Do you see your relationship with God as more important and dear to you than anything else in your life?

■ ■ ■

■ ■ ■

"I will build My church, and the gates

of Hades shall not prevail against it"

(Matthew 16:18 NKJV).

■ ■ ■

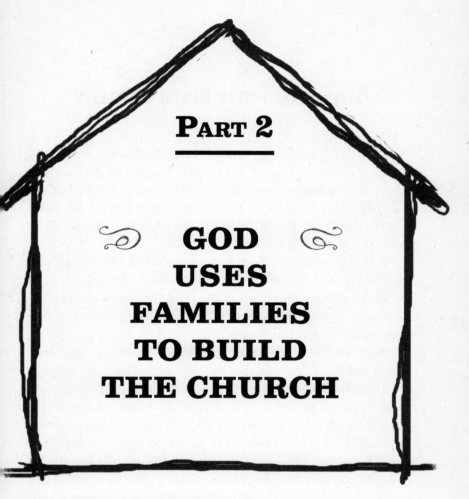

PART 2

GOD USES FAMILIES TO BUILD THE CHURCH

GOD USED CHRIST'S FAMILY

*B*ill and Gloria Gaither wrote a familiar song with lyrics that began, "I'm so glad I'm a part of the Family of God; I've been washed in the fountain, cleansed by His Blood!"

We've sung this song for generations, and it reminds us there's more to the church than mere religious association; we're family—brothers and sisters in Christ.

Let's look more closely at how God used family to build the church. He used Christ's family and extended family. God made the family concept important in the New Testament and particularly to the church, the body of Christ. God also provides for balance between home and church.

The New Testament begins with the record of a young couple, Joseph and Mary, learning they were about to have a son through the miraculous intervention of God's Holy Spirit. The family God chose to raise His Son was humble, hardworking, and of simple means. They faced immediate challenges that required quick action by Joseph to ensure the survival of his young bride and their new son. Without his simple faith and timely obedience to God, the life of the Messiah would have been in jeopardy (Matthew 2:16). This couple, together with several brothers and sisters, nurtured Jesus and provided the security and love every child needs. Though the Bible gives little information about Jesus's relationship with His family or relatives, interesting details come to light when we dig deeper.

Jesus's parents honored God in their lives before they married. The Bible describes Joseph as a "righteous" man (Matthew 1:19); this was his reputation in the community. He was kind and honorable, initially not wanting to disgrace Mary by breaking off their engagement. His willingness to follow God's direction to marry

Mary demonstrated courage and fear of the Lord, as it would change his life's direction and bring tremendous responsibility upon him.

His fiancée Mary also was one who sought God, as the angel described her as "full of grace" or "highly favored" and said, "The Lord is with you" (Luke 1:28). Despite her youth, she demonstrated incredible humility and responsiveness to God as well as great courage in accepting the incredible assignment from God. Likewise, 33 years later, she began to come to grips with the course of events that led her firstborn Son to the Cross.

Joseph and Mary were exemplary in their individual lives; together they were just what God sought in a couple to parent His Son. Spiritually, they were not only able to clearly discern God's direction to them, but also they were immediately obedient and willing to follow God, regardless of the cost. Joseph encountered God in dreams and visions (Matthew 1:20; 2:12–13, 19) whereas Mary encountered the angel Gabriel face-to-face (Luke 1:26–38). There was no question that they had encountered God and about what He had asked them to do.

We know this family had high regard for God and for His Word. They followed God's commands—circumcision, naming Jesus, dedicating Him, taking Him to observe the Passover annually—in line with Deuteronomy 6 and their role in encouraging young Jesus's obedience and devotion. They would have recited how God intervened in their lives, faithfully protected them, and led them through dangerous and difficult times. At age 12, Jesus demonstrated His supernatural understandings and ability to debate with religious leaders (Luke 2:46), as well as obedience to the father and mother who nurtured Him.

Family Assignments

In the larger context of family, an angel had already visited Jesus's older relatives before His mother's encounter. Luke 1:11 describes Zacharias's encounter with the angel who announced to him that his wife, Elizabeth, would bear a son and they would name him John. When God looked for a couple to raise this important prophet, there seems to have been none more qualified than

Elizabeth and Zacharias. Luke 1:6 (NKJV) says: "And they were both righteous before God, walking in all the commandments and ordinances of the Lord blameless." It would seem from looking at Joseph and Mary and Zacharias and Elizabeth that when God has in mind to work through families, He first looks for those already seeking *Him*! In some ways, God working through a family is a reward for faithfulness to Him and a natural way for God to work through those who seek Him. It's improbable God would choose to work through those who ignore Him or have chosen to go in their own direction rather than seek God's and His heart's desire for their lives.

There's a pattern throughout the Bible: God calls people whose hearts are sensitive toward Him and then draws them into various assignments He has for them. Often one of the requirements for His servants is that they be seen "righteous" or "just" in His eyes. "For You, O Lord, will bless the righteous; with favor You will surround him as with a shield" (Psalm 5:12 NKJV).

When God searched for a family to carry on the human race He was about to destroy by flood, He didn't have to look far. He found only one man He considered righteous. "Noah was a just man, perfect in his generations. Noah walked with God.... Then the Lord said to Noah, 'Come into the ark, you and your household, because I have seen that you are righteous before Me in this generation'" (Genesis 6:9; 7:1 NKJV).

What people see and what God sees are two different things.

There was a little church building on the corner of Monroe Avenue and Third Street in Saskatoon whose light was about to go out, spiritually and physically. People saw a flat-roofed, white stucco building with a massive crack running diagonally down the side, a front door that wouldn't open all the way because the overhang was drooping too low, and only a dozen or so people left who ventured inside its walls from week to week. But God had an assignment in mind for a willing family who would come and pastor that little church.

God not only saw the 13 people gathered together each week to pray, He also saw a future Bible college, dozens of mission churches planted, hundreds of people called into the ministry, and a book called *Experiencing God* that would have an impact around the world. But it depended on whether the family He chose would be faithful to the task and trust Him, even when things looked very bleak.

There are many such opportunities God has prepared—without respect for person—for people willing to serve. It may be working as a greeter, serving at the church coffee bar, helping a family with a handicapped child, or something else. God is looking for someone willing to go and serve and make all the difference in the lives of others.

Jesus's Extended Family's Assignments

It's instructive to realize Jesus had family members and several relatives who were very much a part of His ministry and who were instrumental in establishing the community of believers that came together after His resurrection and ascension.

- Tradition has it that Jesus's mother, Mary, became an important part of the church in Ephesus—together with the Apostle John, who was possibly her nephew.
- Christ's cousin John (the Baptist) baptized Jesus in the Jordan River and hailed Him as the "Lamb of God who takes away the sin of the world!" (John 1:29 NKJV).
- Jesus's half brother James wrote the New Testament Book of James (Galatians 1:19).
- Jesus's half brother Jude also wrote the short New Testament book named after him (Luke 6:16; Matthew 13:55).
- Many believe at least two of Jesus's disciples, James and John, the sons of Zebedee, could have been first cousins to Christ through their mother Salome, supposedly Mary's sister (John 19:25; Matthew 27:56). This may explain why James and John's mother (probably Jesus's aunt) would ask special privileges from Jesus for her two boys (Matthew 20:20–21).

Having family around would have been a great support to Jesus of Nazareth. Perhaps this gives insight into why James and John were two of His closest disciples and why He spoke so highly of John the Baptist (Matthew 11:11). It's greatly significant to note the reciprocal endorsements given by cousins James, John, and John the Baptist, and half brothers Jude and James, that support Christ as the Messiah. No one would have known Jesus better than His own family, and their acknowledgment of Christ's resurrection and ascension carries a great deal of weight historically.

One of my (Tom) great joys has been to minister alongside my older brother, Richard, once as his associate pastor after I graduated from seminary, and currently in Blackaby Ministries International where I am also able to serve alongside my father. There's a special bond between family members who know each other, trust one another, and know how to support one another in areas of weakness.

Having our father as our pastor meant whatever we did in service to God through the church was a way for us to share in his ministry, and together we were able to see the hand of God at work. My father baptized two of his future daughters-in-law and had another work with him as a summer missionary. He has coauthored at least one book with every one of his children!

Even if you believe you are the first person among your family to follow God, your faithfulness is an incredible blessing to your family, not only today but for generations to come. As we progress through this book, it will become clear how effective families working together can be in God's kingdom and just how important a heritage of faith is.

When Christ finished His earthly ministry and hung on the Cross about to die, one of His very last acts of kindness was toward His mother.

When Jesus therefore saw His mother, and the disciple whom He loved standing by, He said to His mother, "Woman, behold your son!" Then He said to the disciple, "Behold your mother!" And from that hour that disciple took her to his own home" (John 19:26–27 NKJV).

Although there were times in Christ's ministry where it appears He deliberately distanced Himself from His own mother, sisters, and brothers, He was still Mary's firstborn son. One of His duties was to ensure the care of His mother after He was no longer able to fulfill that role. Family mattered to Him right to the end.

His physical body transformed into a glorified body after the Resurrection, Christ was then able to spiritually reside, or abide, in each person who surrendered to His lordship. The people of God emerged as His new family and body. Each one who would do the will of His Father in heaven would be a member (Matthew 12:50). ☐

GOD BEGAN CHURCHES WITH FAMILIES

*A*fter Christ's ascension, those who began to gather in His name became the church—the *ekklesia*—"called-out ones." Called out from the world, synagogues, idolatrous temple worship, from lives of sin. Called together by God's Spirit who acted as their leader, guide, and teacher, and using the apostles' eyewitness accounts of Christ and their recounting of all He had taught them.

A Greek word normally reserved for families and households, *oikos*, was quickly applied to the new fledgling groups of believers who gathered in Christ's name. Initially, they were not called Christians, but followers of "the Way" (Acts 9:2; 19:9). It was these followers that Paul went to destroy in Damascus that glorious day he met Jesus. He was likely headed to Ananias's house to arrest him, as Ananias was a leader among Jesus's followers. When

Ananias came to return Saul's sight, as Jesus had commanded him to do, the one who was blinded was able to truly see for the first time in his life. He humbly accepted God's commission to begin churches among the Gentiles (non-Jews) and to spend the rest of his life strengthening those he once sought to destroy.

Paul demonstrated *his* compassion for families when believers in Troas gathered in a home to hear him speak. They met on the top floor of the house where Paul ate with them and reasoned with them late into the night (Acts 20). While the adults were listening intently to Paul, a young boy named Eutychus fell fast asleep while sitting on a windowsill and tragically fell to his death. Paul had the boy brought to him, and then gave him back, alive and well, to his family. That home was never the same again! The power of God's Word was not only spoken, but also demonstrated. I (Tom) grew up in a pastor's home and my bedroom was in the basement directly below the living room. I can't tell you how many times I fell asleep while my father's voice resonated as he shared the living Word of God late into the night with people in need of God's power in their lives. I could sympathize with Eutychus!

> TEACHABLE MOMENTS ARE OPPORTUNITIES TO EXPLAIN GOD AND THE CHRISTIAN LIFE TO OUR CHILDREN IN AN INTENTIONAL WAY, A WAY THAT ALSO WILL INFLUENCE FUTURE GENERATIONS.

Families played a significant role in the Apostle Paul's ministry. We don't know all the circumstances, but on at least three occasions, Paul led entire families to the Lord and baptized them. God often touches one person's heart with the intention of reaching his or her entire family. Once the family sees the genuine transformation Christ makes in a person's life, they have to find out more. Many times in the Bible and today, when one family member comes to Christ, it won't be long until the entire family responds to God's love.

Henry Blackaby tells about the ministry in his family while growing up: "We were transferred to British Colombia, right next to the Alaskan border. Where I lived was a difficult place to grow up. I was there 11 years. It was the end of the railway; it was a mining, logging, and fishing camp; a native Indian shipping center; and it was a place of concentrated sin. My layman father was thrust into the midst of that. He worked as a branch manager for the Bank of Montreal and served as chairman of the chamber of commerce. He was involved in the community and was a well-respected businessman. But his heart was to bring people to Christ.

"Although he was a prestigious businessman in the community, he was also a man of integrity who rented a dance hall for a church and preached the gospel to the lost. He was a man who functioned by principle rather than by position as a bank manager, and gave bank loans based more on character than on credit history. He desired to live out his life as an authentic Christian and businessman and each year would bring home homeless people for the family Christmas meal.

"When we started that church in Prince Rupert, my father preached, my mother played the piano, my older brother ushered, and my younger brother and I were the congregation! I can still remember my father, as he would print out those little titles for his message. The sign outside the dance hall said, 'Christ Crucified, Crowned, and Coming,' then listed his sermon topic. For about eight months there was just our family at the service.

"One night a 21-year-old man stumbled in. My father used to say, 'Open those back doors. Mother, play that piano a little louder. Boys, let's sing. There might be a poor lost sinner coming by and hear us singing "Jesus Saves" and come in and be saved.' So we sang a little louder and suddenly in walked this poor guy. He was kind of broken and disheartened. He sat down and Dad preached as he had never preached before.

"At the invitation, my dear father said, 'Let's close our eyes.' Then I heard him say, 'If there is anybody here tonight who wants to accept Jesus Christ as your Savior, will you raise your hand?' Then I heard my father's voice cry and he said, 'Praise God, there is one who wants to be saved.' Well, we knew who that one was. That young man was saved that night. Over time, I watched God establish a church in that town that remains to this day."

House Churches

In the New Testament there were no church buildings on the street corners, no steeples with bells chiming the start of church services, no crosses placed outside of structures identifying them as places of worship for believers of "the Way." The primary reason most of the churches in the Book of Acts began in the private homes of believers was for expediency and for safety. When Saul of Tarsus had begun his hunt to eradicate Christians, he had used a systematic, calculated approach. "But Saul began to destroy the church. Going from house to house, he dragged off men and women and put them in prison" (Acts 8:3 NIV).

After Paul's (formerly Saul) conversion and missionary travels throughout Asia Minor, he wrote letters of encouragement and instruction to these very house churches.

- Rome: "Likewise greet the church that is in their house" (Romans 16:5 NKJV).
- Corinth: "The churches of Asia greet you. Aquila and Priscilla greet you heartily in the Lord, with the church that is in their house" (1 Corinthians 16:19 NKJV).
- Colossae: "Greet the brethren who are in Laodicea, and Nymphas and the church that is in his house" (Colossians 4:15 NKJV).
- Colossae: "to the beloved Apphia, Archippus our fellow soldier, and to the church in your house" (Philemon 1:2 NKJV).

The wealthier members among the believers would have opened their homes as a meeting place and as a guesthouse for traveling apostles, elders, or church leaders. Paul speaks to Philemon who had opened his home for church meetings, "Prepare a guest room for me, for I trust that through your prayers I shall be granted to you" (Philemon 1:22 NKJV).

The fact that churches were so closely tied to homes is not without significance. Again, the members of these newly formed bodies of Christ were functioning as spiritual families for one another. They were enduring official persecution by the Roman government as well as unofficial harassment and persecution by fellow Jews who denied the claims of Jesus as Messiah. Believers clung together in homes that were places of safety, warmth, and encouragement.

Many people today may not realize these homes were not what Westerners would know as typical houses. Archaeologists have determined that Roman and Corinthian houses big enough for a church meeting would have included a large, walled, colonnaded garden or courtyard within the property. These open areas often sported fishponds or pools that could be used for baptisms and washing and were separate from sleeping quarters and other rooms. As many as 100 or more people could assemble in some of these areas. The early house churches could have easily surpassed the average size of some established churches in the Western world today!

Philippi: A seller of cloth and a prison guard

Paul and Silas went to the city of Philippi, capital in the province of Macedonia (Acts 16). It had been founded by Augustus as a Roman colony in 42 B.C. The missionary duo heard of believers meeting down by the river for prayer. There they met Lydia, a businesswoman, who heard Paul speaking and accepted Christ. The Bible tells us her entire household was baptized that day (Acts 16:15). Out of gratitude, she insisted the two evangelists use her home as theirs while in Philippi. As they continued to share the gospel message, they caused no small disturbance. The authorities took exception to their message and had them stripped, beaten, and thrown into prison. The Bible describes it as a severe beating. They were put into the inner prison, with their legs fastened into leg irons.

Their jailer heard Paul and Silas praying and singing hymns to God late into the night. Perhaps he laughed at their behavior, thinking that surely they would come to understand the gravity of their situation soon. Then the earthquake struck, shaking every prisoner free. Thinking he was losing his charges and his job, the jailer pulled his sword to take his own life. Paul assured him they were all present and accounted for, saving the jailer's life, but it was the jailer's soul Paul had his sights on. Paul and Silas's faithfulness and confidence in the midst of severe adversity had won over their captor. Acts 16:30–34 (NKJV) tells us:

> And he brought them out and said, "Sirs, what must I do to be saved?" So they said, "Believe on the Lord Jesus Christ, and you will be saved, you and your household." Then they spoke the word of the Lord to him and to all who were in his house. And he took them the same hour of the night and washed their stripes. And immediately he and all his family were baptized. Now when he had brought them into his house, he set food before them; and he rejoiced, having believed in God with all his household.

What we find moving here is that this brutal, stone-hearted guard cared so much about his family that he would awaken them in the night to hear about Jesus! He would have been chosen for his job as chief jailer because he had both the personality and the physical means to carry out any sentence handed down by the magistrates. No doubt he was an intimidating figure.

No one knows all that God is doing in peoples' hearts. Perhaps this jailer had seen so much death that he was searching for meaning in life. Maybe he felt isolated and forgotten in a stench-filled, rat-infested prison. Racked with guilt over what he had done to others that he didn't want to continue living. The jailer saw something in Paul and Silas that impressed him as worth having. How could two men be so committed, defiant, confident, and sure of themselves after having been beaten mercilessly? Incredible!

We doubt his family had ever seen a prisoner in their home, much less taken part in cleaning and bandaging wounds their father had inflicted. Then the family fed the apostles a meal and listened to them share about Jesus of Nazareth: how He had lived, was crucified by Roman soldiers, and was raised to life by God. Each person in the family believed that night.

Had they ever seen their father so excited about anything? They could have looked at their born-again father and asked, "OK, who are *you* and what have you done with our *real* father?" We suspect his encounter with Paul and Silas that night ruined him as a jailer forever. We can picture him at worship services, serving as a smiling usher, guarding the door, and protecting his new friends. Incredible!

The jailer's family would become pillars in the church in Philippi with Lydia's family. What a story they could tell of meeting Paul and Silas and the transformation that took place in their father's life and their own.

Corinth: A committed couple and a synagogue ruler

Corinth was an ancient city in Greece about 40 miles from Athens, a port city known for its wealth and the luxurious, immoral, and idolatrous lifestyle of its people. Here Paul, together with a husband and wife named Aquila and Priscilla (also known as Prisca), shared the gospel of Christ with great passion. Initially, Paul taught weekly in the local synagogue; and then after Silas and young Timothy arrived (Acts 18:5), Paul devoted his time to preaching about Christ. Crispus, the ruler of the synagogue, was cut to the heart with his message and was converted to Christ. Crispus, in good conscience, was no longer allowed to function in his role as synagogue ruler after his conversion, for verse 17 tells us he was replaced by Sosthenes.

Not only did Crispus believe Paul's message, but the Bible tells us that his entire household came to Christ (Acts 18:8) and was baptized together. Many others in the city came to Christ, both Jews and Gentiles, but Crispus's family would become central to the fledgling Corinthian church. "Then Crispus, the ruler of the synagogue, believed on the Lord with his whole household. And many of the Corinthians, hearing, believed and were baptized" (Act 18:8 NKJV). It's believed Crispus also would later become the bishop of Aegina (a city in Greece), giving encouragement and guidance to many believers.

Paul had families on his heart; he also mentions baptizing Stephanas's family in his letter to the Corinthian church (1 Corinthians 1:16). What's interesting about Stephanas's family is its devotion to the cause of Christ and the impact it had on Paul's ministry personally.

> I urge you, brethren—you know the household of Stephanas, that it is the firstfruits of Achaia, and that they have devoted themselves to the ministry of the saints—that you also submit to such, and to everyone who works and labors with us. I am glad about the coming of Stephanas, Fortunatus, and Achaicus, for what was lacking on your part they supplied. For they refreshed my spirit and yours. Therefore acknowledge such men (1 Corinthians 16:15–18 NKJV).

Here Paul speaks of Stephanas's family as an integral part of the church ministry and to him personally. *Achaia* was a Roman term for Greece, where the church in Corinth was located. We suspect Fortunatus and Achaicus were two members of Stephanas's family and they journeyed together to Rome to minister to Paul during his incarceration. What a great example of how families can serve together. We don't have the details of how they cared for Paul, but it seems he was in great need of encouragement from the family of faith and probably some financial assistance to pay his bills while he awaited trial.

Paul also speaks of Chloe's family (1 Corinthians 1:11), who had visited with Paul and had informed him there were divisions and dissension among the church members in Corinth. Paul doesn't identify who these family members were. Regardless, Chloe's family had a vested interest in unity among the members. They were concerned enough about bickering and competition within the church that they went for outside help when they were not able to manage things on their own. This is a commendable action on behalf of a family who wants to protect its church family from the inevitable distraction, division, and destruction that accompany unresolved arguments.

Caesarea: An evangelist and his daughters

Caesarea was built by Herod the Great in 10 B.C. and was located on the road from Tyre to Egypt, about 70 miles northwest of Jerusalem. On one of Paul's journeys, he and Luke visited Philip the evangelist in Caesarea. This was the Philip chosen as one of the first seven deacons in the early church (Acts 8) and who, along with Stephen, stood out as one "full of the Holy Spirit and wisdom." He was the first to preach to the Samaritans and demonstrated God's miraculous powers among them (Acts 8:5–13). The Spirit led him to an encounter with a high-ranking Ethiopian eunuch whom he led to the Lord on the road to Gaza.

By the time of Paul's missionary travels, Philip had settled in Caesarea with his wife and family (Acts 21:8–9). We know of his four daughters because Luke, the author of Acts, took note of them as being unmarried and as having the gift of prophecy or inspired teaching. We must assume that Philip and his wife had a God-centered home where all the family members were a part of their father's ministry and contributed to the effort of equipping God's people and sharing the good news of the gospel to the unsaved. We would expect their church to have quite an outstanding discipleship ministry with four qualified and Spirit-led women teaching the truths of the kingdom of God under the watch-care of a famous evangelist dad. No wonder Paul felt welcome in their home!

It must have been quite a fascinating visit for Paul to speak with Philip. The Bible records that Philip was the first believer to take the gospel to the Gentiles as Paul was later commissioned to do. Paul would have had a wonderful time fellowshipping with Philip's family and sharing with them all he and his companions had seen in his travels. Paul would later return to Caesarea, but not as a preacher compelled by the love of God; he would be a prisoner constrained by Roman guards. For the next two years, Paul waited in a prison before being extradited to Rome and he would have appreciated all the encouragement Philip's family and church could offer (Acts 23–26).

In many cities, it was the family who formed the bedrock of the early church. The family provided a place to meet, evangelized and taught, cared for others, worked for unity, and led their families to know and serve God. □

BALANCING CHURCH AND FAMILY TODAY

When the first churches were started, they had to be properly established to ensure their survival and growth. The Apostle Paul took great pains to help new believers understand the gospel message and appreciate their new relationship with one another. They were to treat one another with great care, as Christ would have treated them. Paul wrote to young pastor Timothy, instructing him in how to choose leaders who would care for the body of Christ, the church. In his letter, Paul insisted that when considering a man for leadership, a careful check on how well he has led his own family was a prerequisite. "He must manage his own family well and see that his children obey him with proper respect. (If anyone does not know how to manage his own family, how can he take care of God's church?)" (1 Timothy 3:4–5 NIV).

According to this passage, the measure by which we are able to properly lead and manage our own family will be the measure by which we are able to lead and manage those in God's family. Although the position of bishop (Greek—*episkopos*) or overseer is mentioned here, this can equally apply to those who have spiritual oversight over others, or are in positions of leadership. In effect, those who are giving oversight to God's people need to have their own house in order before they are given places of responsibility in the church or in a ministry.

These two verses in 1 Timothy have rather large implications for the church and for the family.

1. The Importance of the Family in Relation to the Church

The verse does *not* tell us that children should have great respect and admiration for their father or mother because he or she holds the title of deacon or elder or pastor or teacher in the church. It does *not* say whatever responsibilities you have at church should take priority over what is done in the home. It says the church should respect people and allow them to have leadership *because* of how well they have first demonstrated exceptional leadership with their spouse and children in the home. One's relationship with his or her spouse and with his or her children is exceedingly important; in fact, it could be used to determine whether or not a person is qualified to serve as a leader in the church. How we relate to our family members speaks to our Christian character.

I was absolutely thrilled when my wife, Kim, and I had our first child, and deeply humbled when the second and third children were born. As a father, I discovered how demanding and self-centered a seven-pound bundle of joy can be! Walking the hallways in the wee hours of the morning with a screaming baby in my ear was *not* what I signed up for!

Yet God began to shape and mold my character through the sleepless nights, the messes, the spit-up down the back of my shoulder, the breaking of precious figurines, and the frustration of not knowing how to console a screaming child. I found that I grew more patient, understanding, gentle, giving, disciplined, and less selfish over the years. There were certain things I could put up with simply because of my deep love for my children that I might not put up with in other circumstances.

It *is* true that "love will cover a multitude of sins" (1 Peter 4:8 NKJV). I look at my teenagers now and know that, as they've grown physically over the years, I've grown in character, insight, and understanding, all of which God uses as I serve Him, and as I serve His people as a fellow traveler walking alongside them in life.

The truth is, God's people can also be stubborn and difficult. They can make messes of their lives. They also can be demanding and unreasonable. They can be inconsolable, selfish, critical, obstinate, and even furious at times. They are like sheep that need a shepherd (Mark 6:34). Learning how to lovingly discipline our children, how to communicate with one another at home, and how to differentiate between emotional responses and rational responses all greatly helped prepare my wife and me for ministry among God's people.

Kim was away on a women's retreat and I was in charge of my two young children for the weekend. My five-year-old son had a stubborn streak and regularly tried to assert his will over mine. Well, we had some differences of opinion that left him wishing it had been Kim watching him rather than me.

Kim's parents lived about an hour away from us at the time. Their phone rang and a little voice on the other end said, "Granny, will you come and get me? Mom is gone and left me with the parent I don't like!" Raising children to be respectful and honoring to their parents has been a challenge over the years, but well worth the effort in the end.

Having served as volunteers or staff in churches for more than 25 years, we've served pastorally, taught small groups, led retreats, guided committees, developed ministries, and counseled many. We've often surveyed a difficult situation with a church member and looked at one another with that "They are just sheep!" look, and sought to provide guidance as a loving shepherd would guide his own flock (family).

2. The Church Body Must Be Protected

Those who seek positions of influence without having a proper understanding or ability to lead God's people should not be given responsibilities over people in the church, no matter how desperate the church may be. People come into leadership for all sorts of reasons, many of which are noble; but sometimes there are ulterior motives that come from pride, manipulation, or the need for power, influence, or worse. A solid family life can indicate the integrity and character needed for guiding God's people.

As a father, I am extremely sensitive to any dubious people or dangerous situations that may affect my family. I wouldn't say I'm overly protective, but I wouldn't hesitate to intervene in any situation where my wife or children may be at risk. Neighborhood bullies, obnoxious people, unreasonable coaches, and overly risky activities all make my radar ping and I jump into ready-for-action mode. On more than one occasion, I've volunteered to drive when I didn't sense the school's designated driver was competent driving in winter conditions. I've volunteered to go on school trips or act as assistant coach on occasions where I felt leaders needed a little help or lacked necessary experience. In essence, I monitor those who have authority over my children, such as coaches, teachers, and youth workers, to be sure they are competent and trustworthy of the responsibility they've been given.

There have been occasions where, as pastor, I've removed people from leadership or ministry positions because they were either ineffective or outright damaging in leading a Sunday School class or other ministry activity. I've been in three churches that have removed people from leadership and membership because of unrepentant and ongoing sin in their lives and the damage they were doing to the church family. I've also restricted visitors' access to church members' activities when those visitors obviously brought destructive agendas. Placing competent leaders in charge demonstrates care and concern for those led and serves the church body.

3. A Parent's Primary Responsibility Is to the Home

God's priority is for church leaders to be spiritual leaders in the home first and, out of that, to be better able to lead God's people. How many committees, ministries, and organizations are led by people who have failed miserably as leaders in their own homes and yet are placed in positions of authority and leadership over God's people?

- A man whose marriage is on the rocks and whose teenage children have gone wild and rebellious continues to serve as an elder.
- A woman divorced three times is leading the women's ministry.
- A pastor whose wife has left him because he spends too much time "married to the church" is allowed to continue as pastor.
- A father who is not on speaking terms with his adult children runs the weekly visitation ministry.
- Children and wives who live in constant fear of an overbearing and demanding father watch him intimidating and threatening others at church to get his own way.
- Parents who have trouble tithing or giving generously to the church are asked to be on the finance committee.

My (Tom) parents raised five children with an age span of nine years between the oldest and youngest. My father was pastoring, starting mission churches, speaking internationally, and running a Bible college all at the same time. His schedule became quite ridiculous at times. Feeling a bit neglected (as second-born children often do), I decided to press the point with my father, and called his secretary one day to make an appointment after school with him. I rode my bicycle to the church that day and his secretary announced that his 3:30 appointment had come. When he opened his door, the look on his face was priceless. He said something about, as his son, my not needing to make appointments, and I replied something about apparently an appointment was the only way I could spend time with him. In the coming months he made a greater effort to come to our soccer games and be more available as our father.

One well-known speaker and figure in the Christian community was once asked how she was able to maintain a balance between her family life and speaking career. She replied, "Oh, balanced people never accomplish anything!" In many ways she is right. The goal in life is not to have balance, but to have one's priorities in the right place. If our priorities are correctly aligned, then the investment of our time and resources will follow.

We reap what we sow. This is a farming axiom and spiritual

principle that the Bible teaches. "Do not be deceived, God is not mocked; for whatever a man sows, that he will also reap" (Galatians 6:7 NKJV). Another word for sowing in modern terminology is *investing*. It's never a bad idea to invest in our marriage and in our children as we will reap tremendous rewards in the coming years. We are not talking about financial investment, per se, but spiritual investment, time investment, emotional investment—investments that will last for eternity.

Godly families generally produce godly children who most often turn into godly adults. By the mercy and grace of God, there are wonderful examples of godly people coming from dysfunctional and destructive families. And sadly, there are children of godly parents who rebel and choose to turn their backs on God. But as a general rule, where we invest our lives will determine what sort of dividends or fruit we receive. Parents who invest in their family will have a family who loves them and supports them when family is all they have left. Those who live for their job, career, and money come to the end of life and find they are strangers to their own wife and children.

Many Christians feel it spiritual to sacrifice their family for the sake of ministry. In many ways there is sacrifice involved in living out one's Christian life. We must give up what we may like to do or have in order to gain much more in God's kingdom. However, sacrificing our family time, resources, interests, or unity at the expense of doing good at church should be an *exception*, not a rule.

At times there may be valid reasons to miss the occasional family night, concert, or game, or to put family vacation money toward worthy causes. However, this should be a family decision, not a unilateral decision Dad or Mom makes on a regular basis. When our children realize we won't be home for their special time with us because we are ministering to a person in need, they can pray for us and we can report back how their prayers helped us help another.

When as a family we decide to give our vacation fund to help victims of disaster or crisis in the name of Jesus, children can see how their sacrifice will make a difference too. By including the family in the decision-making process, family members participate willingly in the sacrifice, and together rejoice in the ministry. Resentment can build if parents regularly neglect the needs of their own family in order to serve others. This resentment can extend not only to parents but also to the church.

A pastor's son recently told me the sad truth that his father never sat down with him or any of his siblings and explained the plan of salvation to them! He was pretty good at sharing with others, but he never took the time to care for his own children's spiritual lives.

What profit is there to having a great ministry or fulfilling Bible study or strong outreach programs in the community if our own children and spouse are neglected and in jeopardy of turning away from God? There are numerous pastors and church leaders who, if they could do it all over again, would do things differently.

The last two churches in which we served interviewed me (Tom) before my coming on staff. In both cases I told them this: "If I come on staff in this church, I want you to know that if there is ever a major calendar conflict between my family and the church, my family will win. I may serve in many churches over the years, but I only have one family to raise." The senior pastor in one church and the chairman of deacons in the other church both said to me afterwards, "What you said about your family commitment is a nice thought, but it isn't realistic." And I replied, "Just watch me." Over the next 13 years of ministry in those two churches, I kept that promise!

Kim and I believe church leaders who demonstrate to their congregations that their marriage and their family come first after God can be a tremendous blessing to other families. People who have not learned to distinguish church from God have trouble with this. Loving God with all our heart, soul, strength, and mind is not the same as being at every church event!

Reasons to Focus on the Family

Much has been said here about the priority of the home. We don't mean to undermine the importance of the church; rather we seek to bring a proper balance and perspective between the two. Without a significant investment in one's children, it will be very difficult to serve together as a family. The church cannot function properly without strong families to support it, and the family cannot accomplish all that God intends without a strong church supporting it.

Here are a few final thoughts in developing a strong spiritual foundation in the home.

1. Children Will Catch the Passion

Children often develop the same passions their parents possess. It may be a particular sport or hobby, a political position, or community involvement. The list is long. The relationship parents have with God can easily be "caught" by their children also. When children watch their parents love and serve God, they will want to love and serve God, particularly when parents involve the children in ministry activities. It's easy to see how Abraham's faith impressed his son Isaac's faith, and how Isaac's faith affected Jacob's faith, or how Philip's daughters followed in his footsteps, or how easy it was for Stephanas's two sons, Fortunatus and Achaicus, to travel to Rome with their dad to minister to Paul. Maybe you've heard the old saying, "Faith is better caught than taught"? This is what it means. The relationship a mother and father have with God should always be lived out in the home first so it can have a significant impact outside of the home.

2. Investing in Children Means Investing in the Future

The spiritual investments we make today in our children can reap amazing benefits in the future. Many straying and wayward children of church families could have been redeemed if parents had taken a break from ministry the moment they saw their children heading into trouble. Had they used the time spent doing good things outside the home to walk with their children in the home with love and grace, the children may have been turned around and avoided tremendous pain and sorrow.

Here is a great verse to remember when parenting (though it's written concerning salvation): "For by grace you have been saved through faith, and that not of yourselves; it is the gift of God, not of works, lest anyone should boast" (Ephesians 2:8–9 NKJV). We say we believe we are saved through *faith*, and then *act* like we are saved through *works*! Instead, we can model for our children lives of faith and grace, and the works will come in due time. Yet, if we model lives of works, we may find that faith and grace may never show up.

David describes his family this way, "One's relationship with God and obedience to Him was without a doubt the most important thing in our home. There was no question of that with my parents. They are very generous people and have supported missionaries and church workers over the years. Dad is a hands-on servant, willing to do manual labor at the church and for others, which is probably what he enjoys doing most.

"The importance of the Bible was imprinted on my brother and me as well. I remember attending a church that did not have Bible Drills, so my mother started a chapter because she felt it was so important that the youth were memorizing Scripture.

"They have been very supportive over the years and willing to speak truth whenever needed. My mother and my father both want to keep me in line with God; and if they think I am following my own will, being selfish, or not praying enough about something, they will tell me. They are willing to ask me the hard questions and be honest with me, and I think that is important for parents to do, especially when you are a teenager. Instead of just telling me what to do, they taught me to seek God for myself." □

FAMILY-TIME
REFLECTIONS

1. Can you list your top six priorities?

2. Do your time and resource investments reflect the same order that you have listed?

3. Relist your priorities in the order of your time and resource investments.

4. What steps will you make to reprioritize to reflect your true priorities?

5. What outcomes do you hope for?

■ ■ ■

■ ■ ■

Even the sparrow has found a home,

and the swallow a nest for herself,

where she may have her young—

a place near your altar,

O Lord Almighty,

my King and my God.

Blessed are those who dwell

in your house;

they are ever praising you.

Selah

(Psalm 84:3–4 NIV).

■ ■ ■

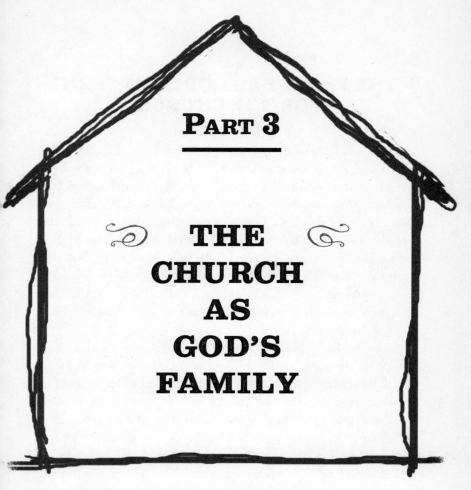

PART 3

THE CHURCH AS GOD'S FAMILY

The Family as God's Pattern for the Church

Families Extend the Mission of the Church

Strengthening Families

Family-Time Reflections

THE FAMILY AS GOD'S PATTERN
FOR THE CHURCH

*P*aul learned early about abandonment, divorce, drugs, and self-reliance. His dad left his family when Paul was five. His mom self-medicated with prescription drugs and later alcohol and was emotionally and physically unavailable to her two young boys for days at a time. Though Paul tried to bond with his father over the years, every effort was rebuffed or ignored. Paul and his brother sought out the Big Brother association; but after several Big Brothers moved on, the disillusioned boys refused to invest emotionally in those who might abandon them. And their years growing up in government housing were challenging and at times overwhelming.

But God had a plan for Paul and began working in his heart. At God's prompting, he and his brother made their way to a local church by getting up early Sundays to catch the bus an hour before church started. Though Paul's brother would later give up on God and the church, Paul kept going. Even though the teenagers at church could be merciless, criticizing Paul's lack of biblical knowledge, he persisted in his search for God.

A loving English teacher named Marg took an interest in Paul. She saw this young man's potential when no one else seemed to care. Unbeknownst to either, they found out they attended the same church. Abandoned by his father, neglected by his mother, ostracized by his youth group, and at odds with his brother, Paul found a *spiritual* mother who refused to abandon him. Paul found a heavenly Father who loved and stood by him. When both of his parents had passed away, it was the godly teacher at church who remained as family for Paul.

Paul now serves on a church staff as a minister to children and he and his wife have adopted two orphans from Africa in an effort to give others what Paul himself had not experienced—an earthly family. Paul's five children have a home where God is the center, and *spiritual* brothers and sisters at church who love them.

God never intended His people to be orphans. According to 1 Peter 1:23 and John 3:3, we are *born again* when we come alive spiritually, able to experience God's presence in our lives and understand spiritual truth. The church is a family, the community for believers to gather in the name of Christ, drawn together by His Spirit for worship, discipleship, and service. Church becomes an immediate support network for believers, providing spiritual family members with whom new believers can fellowship and participate. In fact, growing up as a pastor's kid, the church became my second home.

Church was where we met friends, found prayer support, arranged first dates, and began to find out how God had gifted us for His service. In the early days we arrived an hour before Sunday School to mop up the water that had seeped into the basement from a cracked floor, so classes could meet without getting wet feet. At other times we carried wood and nails for additions we built onto the church. And we became ushers, greeters, choir and committee members, worship leaders and musicians, student preachers, and more over the years. It's impossible to measure the impact our church family has had on us.

Now as parents we see the benefits to our children. Our oldest son learned to play the drums at church, playing for praise teams and in the high school band. My daughter helped in children's programs, learning how to guide children, and also becoming a popular babysitter. She also sings and plays the piano in worship. They both learned leadership skills in the church youth program and serve on missions teams, praise teams, summer kids clubs, and other service venues at church. Our youngest son loves church too; he's always ready before the rest of us on Sundays. Most of all, our kids have learned to love God's people and let them into their lives.

Not everyone has experienced church as a family. Not everyone has found a place to use their gifts, or be involved in significant ways. Sometimes churches struggle to create a sense of family among their membership and relationships seem distant and impersonal. For Paul, it took one person to draw him in and help him feel connected to a church family. Every person can take the initiative to draw others into the family of God.

The church is first and foremost the body of Christ (Romans 12:5; 1 Corinthians 12:27). Every person who is a part of a church is related to all other Christians through Jesus, the head of the body (Ephesians 5:23). Each person plays a role in the life and ministry of the church body; and when any member does not function as Christ intended, the rest are spiritually dysfunctional in some capacity. Like a family, when one member is sick, hurt, or struggling, the household is affected. In our household, when Mom is sick, the whole family has to adjust because she's at the center of our home life!

God masterfully intertwines His activities and purposes together throughout time, giving us vivid parallels between *family* life and the *church* body's life. From the very beginning, God intended that the way in which He related to mankind would be the way we should relate to one another. The same sacrificial love God showed Adam was to be shown by Adam to his wife, Eve. The same selfless love Adam and Eve had for one another would then be shown to their children in their home. The *agape* love family members show one another should also be shown toward other believers in Christ's body.

God's people are to function in the church as God intended, relating as brothers and sisters in Christ. God's relationship with His people is to be reflected in the family and in the church. God demonstrated His love for us: "For God loved the world so much that he gave his only Son, so that everyone who believes in him may not die but have eternal life" (John 3:16 GNT). God tells us how to love: "And God showed his love for us by sending his only Son into the world, so that we might have life through him.... Dear friends, if this is how God loved us, then we should love one another" (1 John 4:9, 11 GNT). Jesus Himself commands us: "My commandment is this: love one another, just as I love you. The greatest love you can have for your friends is to give your life for them" (John 15:12–13 GNT).

- God's demonstration of love to us shows us how to love our family and friends.
- When a father wants to know how to lead his family, he only has to look at the way God led His people.
- When a man wants to know how to treat his wife, he can look at how Christ gave His life for His church.
- The same sacrificial love that was shown on the Cross can be shown by a mother to her children, and can be seen as people care for one another in the church.
- The same protection, nurturing, sustenance, and guidance God provided His chosen people is to be shown daily by parents toward their children and in the church by its leaders toward the flock.

Unfortunately, as the family is flawed, so is the church. There's compassion, grace, forgiveness, sacrificial love, and acts of kindness as well as complaining, bickering, backstabbing, criticism, and selfishness among God's people. The same imperfections seen in families are also common in the church. As Christians, we have access to the Holy Spirit who works in us to help us forgive, exhort, rebuke, love, and offer grace to one another so we can all grow in love together in Christ.

Richard Blackaby writes regarding difficulties at church: "Lisa and I did address some of the issues in the church at times, but we always tried to think through the issue with our kids and how it might be addressed. We always encouraged our kids to be a part of the solution. For example, when there was a lot of criticism about the music director, I agreed with some of it and talked with my boys about some of my philosophical issues, but then took the boys with me to take the director out for lunch to try and encourage him. As a result, our kids grew up to not necessarily always agree with everything that happened in church but to realize you don't have to like or agree with everything in your church for it to be a good church."

Godly People Influencing Your Family

Many of our heroes were those we met through church. Some were older, seasoned Christians who had dedicated their lives to serve the Lord. Others were vibrant, excited, new Christians who had such a faith-filled outlook on life it was contagious for everyone around them. Many of the veteran Christians, such as pastors, missionaries, and ministers, visited with our father in our home or sat with us at our supper table from time to time. As young people, we were often inspired by their dedication to God, the sacrifices they had made over the years, and by stories of God's faithfulness in the midst of difficult times. Rather than seeing our home as a hideaway or private place, we valued having God's people bless our home and family with their presence, and this has influenced future generations.

Marilynn Blackaby says, "We often invited missionaries into our home for dinner and our children were able to visit with them, ask questions, and hear some pretty amazing stories about God's work around the world. Any family can volunteer to host real-live missionaries, drive them around, or have them over for meals. We also tried to surround our children with people who loved God and that they looked up to such as many of the college students in our church. On more than one occasion the college students would include our children in various outings, such as canoe trips, fund-raising events, leading the worship at mission churches in other towns, and taking our teenagers to student conferences. This had a tremendous impact on their lives and on their understanding of what it meant to be a Christian."

It's valuable to seek out people who have a heart for God and invite them into our homes and lives. They need not be missionaries, pastors, or ministers. They can be ordinary people who love God and enjoy serving Him where they are. The stories they share about God's faithfulness will leave lasting impressions on our children as well as increase parents' faith. Many times such people can influence the direction of our children's lives and inspire them to be faithful in their own walk with God.

Loving God's People

Although Christ was never married, the church was as dear and precious to Him as a wife to a husband, and more so. The intimacy and care between Christ and the church is unmistakably reflected in the most basic human relationship between a husband and wife. Christ not only loved the church, He died for it. "Husbands, love your wives, just as Christ also loved the church and gave Himself for her" (Ephesians 5:25 NKJV).

Peter admonished the church to understand how to demonstrate love for one another: "And above all things have fervent love for one another, for 'love will cover a multitude of sins.' Be hospitable to one another without grumbling. As each one has received a gift, minister it to one another, as good stewards of the manifold grace of God" (1 Peter 4:8–10 NKJV).

However, in many churches today, people put up with each other, work with one another, and serve together, but rarely do members actually love one another as Christ intends. "Is there any encouragement from belonging to Christ? Any comfort from his love? Any fellowship together in the Spirit? Are your hearts tender and sympathetic? Then make me truly happy by agreeing wholeheartedly with each other, loving one another, and working together with one heart and purpose. Don't be selfish; don't live to make a good impression on others. Be humble, thinking of others as better than yourself. Don't think only about your own affairs, but be interested in others, too, and what they are doing" (Philippians 2:1–4 NLT).

Loving others means valuing unity and others' needs over personal opinions and agendas, taking an interest in others' lives regardless of others showing an interest in you. It means encouraging others' accomplishments and rejoicing in their successes. Loving involves serving others and not waiting to be served.

I (Tom) was asked by a pastor how to deal with troublesome church members. I responded with a question, inquiring whether the troublesome members knew their pastor loved them. His response: a blank stare. Many troublesome members are crying out to be loved. Their parents, siblings, or relatives may not love them, but the church is the place where they should be able to receive unconditional love, encouragement, and grace. If people know you love them, they will put up with a lot of things they may disagree about. But if they do not feel loved, they can be very difficult and irritating. Children are the same way. It's not hard to know when children need attention and reminders of how important they are to their parents and to their family.

There would be little hesitation on my part to give my life for Kim and the children, but until we can say the same for our brothers and sisters at church, we have not come to love them to the degree Christ expects. Helping our children love one another is incredibly important. Helping church members love one another deeply will create a church family that draws people!

Helping New Christians Learn to Love

Paul encourages Philemon to view his repentant slave, now a believer, in a new light. "For perhaps he departed for a while for this purpose, that you might receive him forever, no longer as a slave but more than a slave—a beloved brother, especially to me but how much more to you, both in the flesh and in the Lord" (Philemon 1:15–16 NKJV).

Paul had to instruct new believers how to behave in the church and relate to their fellow believers. Those that comprised the church did not "grow up in church." In fact, many had worshipped family idols and sacrificed to the gods. Some of their worship practices, quite immoral by today's standards, were to appease the gods, gain favor pertaining to a business venture, traveling mercies, or to prevent crop failure. There was no sense of family with those who went to the pagan temples. Any favor from the gods could have been seen as at the *expense* of your neighbor.

Paul writes to Timothy, "I hope to come to you shortly; but

if I am delayed, I write so that you may know how you ought to conduct yourself in the house of God, which is the church of the living God, the pillar and ground of the truth" (1 Timothy 3:14–15 NKJV). So Paul describes the character church leaders should have (1 Timothy 3), he talks about how men should act (1 Timothy 2:8), and how women should behave (1 Timothy 2:9–15). He gives instructions on how to care for the elderly members of the church (1 Timothy 5:1–2), for widows (1 Timothy 5:3–6), for slaves (1 Timothy 6:1–2), and for those who were wealthy (1 Timothy 6:17–19). The concept of church as family was new, particularly to Gentile believers who had no knowledge of God and how He worked through His people in the past.

Can you imagine having people who've never been a part of any organized religion show up at your home each week? Perhaps many of them would come from broken homes, or out of a life dependent on drugs or even satanic rituals, simply because they didn't know any better, or because their parents led them into it as children. They would have so many hang-ups and hurdles to overcome in their lives. They would need guidance to know how to experience the power and presence of Christ working through them. Where would you start with them? How would you begin to teach them about the kingdom of God or life with Christ as Lord or the importance of the Bible to daily life? This was Paul's challenge and the challenge of those who opened their homes to these new believers in Christ. Slowly, their code of ethics, morals, relationships, attitudes, and behavior all would begin to reflect their Lord and Savior's ethics, morals, relationships, attitudes, and behavior. The church needed to reshape them from being enemies of Christ to ambassadors for Christ (2 Corinthians 5:20).

When God Adds to the Family

When Christ sends people to His churches, He expects the churches to treat them as they would treat Christ Himself. "I am telling you the truth: whoever receives anyone I send receives me also; and whoever receives me receives him who sent me"

(John 13:20 GNT). What we have to consider as Christ's church is that as He directs the lives of believers, He may be sending them to various churches for good reason.

Erika arrived at the international church in Norway all alone one Sunday. It became quickly apparent to this English congregation that she spoke only Spanish and that she was unfamiliar with church, but had nowhere else to turn. As God had planned it, there were a few people who had lived in Venezuela and could communicate with Erika. She had left her family in Chile to look for work in Europe. She had nowhere to live, no job prospects, and couldn't communicate in Norwegian. The church members quickly found her a place to live with a family that spoke Spanish and began to help her learn the local dialect. Several church members hired her to clean their homes to provide some income. Others helped her navigate government employment agencies and searched the papers for jobs in her area of training. Over the next six months Erika came to know the love of Christ and gave her heart to the Lord. However, she did not find work in her field and returned to her children and husband in Chile. Yet she returned a new person and having experienced how a church can be family both physically and spiritually.

Churches that take seriously their role as spiritual families have an *inclusive* attitude that welcomes all visitors, strangers, the hurting, those who are servants, and those who seek a spiritual home or want simply to connect with fellow believers. Every visitor who comes through the doors is welcomed as a brother and sister in the Lord rather than looked at with suspicion, seen as a potential threat to the status quo, or simply ignored.

Some churches have accepted God's assignment to guide immigrants to assimilate into society and teach English as a second language using a simplified English Bible as their textbook. It is no wonder that many of those they serve come to Christ and become important members of their churches.

Other churches struggle to incorporate new people into their fellowship effectively. There's a big difference between being friendly to visitors and drawing them into the heart and life of the church family. New people often bring new ideas. They some-times even question why things are done a certain way. They may not always agree with the church direction, or seem to constantly compare things with how they were done in their last church! To some people this is threatening, but to others it can be a very exciting time because they see each person as sent by God.

We can have a better understanding of this if we compare new members to older children families adopt into their homes. There will be adjustments made, family traditions taught, expla-nations provided, and a concerted effort at assimilating the newcomer into the family's life. Everyone adjusts—not only the newcomer.

A God-centered church will know that each time new people come into their fellowship two things are happening: (1) God is adding new ideas, skills, gifts, talents, and insights to the body; (2) the church has a new body part to disciple, train, equip, and love. Together, the new member and the body grow into a more complete picture of what God wants His church to be.

The mission statement of First Baptist Church, Biloxi, Mis-sissippi, is "To grow as a Christ-centered family. We believe that a sense of community happens when people experience the change that Jesus alone can make in their lives." This was one of many churches that dealt with the devastation of Hurricane Katrina. More than 100 families in the church lost their homes. They learned quickly the importance of a church family that supports families. They have a loving, discipling, God-centered commu-nity of believers that is helping families serve together on mission around the world and in their own community.

One church in which we served had the motto Friends Becom-ing Family. How do visitors and new members become family? It is more than making a decision to follow Christ and join the church. That might make them family in name, but do they *feel* like family? Feeling like family means a place where

- you are accepted and feel you belong;
- people take an active interest in your life;

- people care for you, help you when you are in need, pray for and look out for you;
- you are given responsibility and can serve;
- you are included and have a contribution to make;
- you are nurtured and fed spiritually. ☐

FAMILIES EXTEND
THE MISSION OF THE CHURCH

*F*amilies who take seriously their relationship with God and their involvement with His people will begin to incorporate the mission of the church as their family mission. This will mean understanding what it means to be servants of God and living that intentionally.

1. The Church Is to Share the Good News of Christ

Everything a church does should have the ultimate goal of bringing people to God. A family that accepts this mission will begin to look for chances to share the gospel in daily life. Going to the park with your preschooler becomes an adventure to see if God has someone there who needs godly friendship. Sitting in the stands at your son's basketball game turns into an opportunity to invite another parent to church. Organizing an outing for your daughter's class, hosting a birthday party in your home, being a driver for the school, or being a volunteer block parent all become ways to connect with people and to see if the Lord has something in mind for you to do as "salt and light" in your community (Matthew 5:13–15). Again, when God saves an individual, He has a whole family in mind and more. Our relationship with God is always meant to be shared, with our family first, and everyone else after that!

Connie, a woman we know, had been running from God for years. She had grown up in a church that was heavy on guilt and light on grace, and the religious rituals she enjoyed as a child no longer appealed to her. Actually, she began to hate everything about church. In 1973, at 18 years old, she headed off to college. To take a break from class work she followed her roommates to an evangelistic crusade in downtown Saskatoon. It was there she encountered a Christian woman who challenged Connie's concept of Christianity and talked with her about a personal relationship with Christ. Connie realized for the first time that God loved her and wanted to be a part of her life; she asked Christ into her heart. She began attending a local church and felt welcomed by the people she met there. The Spirit of God brought instant transformation to many areas of her life and everything about her began to reflect her love for God. Connie began to share her faith with her siblings and soon her younger sister accepted Christ. Together they began having an impact on the others. In the coming years, their youngest sister and her husband were drawn to faith in Christ and now three sisters and their husbands serve God together in the same church.

A seriously disturbed man was living in a graveyard and was a complete wreck physically, emotionally, and spiritually (Mark 5). When Christ released him from satanic bondage and restored him to his right mind, the man determined to devote his life to following Christ. He had a heart to serve the God who had given his life back to him, who had made him whole. Rather than add this new convert to His band of disciples, Jesus instead sent him back to his own family. "However, Jesus did not permit him, but said to him, 'Go home to your friends, and tell them what great things the Lord has done for you, and how He has had compassion on you'" (Mark 5:19 NKJV).

Though many details of this man's life are left out, we surmise he was a grown man who had at least been a son. It's plausible that he had been a devoted father and husband to a young family all but destroyed by his demonic past. It's hard to imagine the pain and embarrassment his family and friends would have experienced, knowing that this man was both feared and derided in their community. Scripture indicates that on several occasions the villagers had tied him up with chains to restrain his bizarre behavior and to minimize the threat he was to passersby, but to no avail. Christ demonstrated compassion and grace to both this man and his family by setting him free. The celebration that took place at his return home must have been something to see, and his testimony indisputable. The graves villagers once feared and avoided were now known as the site where Christ performed a miracle. Jesus gave life and wholeness back to a man and restored a family that had been devastated and broken.

Families and churches work together to bring the good news of Christ's love and sacrifice to those who have not heard it. For many, it starts in the home, sharing with unsaved family members; for other families who are already committed to Christ, they can share with other families who have not yet responded to Christ.

Parents in a family that extends the mission of the church can spend time praying with their children about their unsaved friends. Parents can encourage their children to invite friends to church activities, youth events, children's programs, or Christmas and Easter productions. Have you taught your children the basic steps on how to become a Christian or some good Bible verses to share with those who need Christ? All of these things reflect one of the primary purposes of God's church and His people until He returns.

2. The Church Is to Worship

One of the most important activities of the church is coming together to worship. There are many different ways to worship the Lord God in our homes. We worship Him when we honor His name in our home. Great care is given to not misuse God's name or use it in any meaningless and empty way when talking about Him or talking to Him. The challenge is to help children honor the Lord's name when they hear friends at school, coaches, and other adults in their lives use it flippantly or deliberately take God's name in vain.

We make time for family devotions and prayer. Family devotions have looked very different in our home at various stages in our children's lives. When they were young children, devotions were Bible stories and prayer before bed at night. Devotions later happened best after supper using many different tools and resources designed for families.

> **AS OUR CHILDREN GREW INTO TEENAGERS, THE FIGHT WAS NOT WHETHER OR NOT WE WOULD GO TO CHURCH, BUT WHAT THEY WERE ALLOWED TO WEAR WHEN THEY WENT!**

With busy teenagers we needed to schedule devotions at different times. Topics have been drawn from issues they or their friends may face. At certain stages, daily family devotions may not be feasible. The goal is to inspire our children to want to know God and to apply His Word however that can happen throughout the week.

We worship Him when we have music in our home that praises and honors the Lord. We worship the Lord when we teach our children how to tithe from their income. Giving back to God out of gratefulness for what He has given us is worship that even a child can understand and practice. We worship Him also when we make regular church attendance a priority in our family.

Marilynn Blackaby comments, "We did our best to instill in our children the routine and commitment to be in church on Sundays to worship God. We knew as a family Sunday was a day to worship God. No sleepovers on Saturday night, no year-end team parties, and no sports games or practices would keep us from worship. As our children grew into teenagers, the fight was not whether or not we would go to church, but what they were allowed to wear when they went!"

As a mother with very young children, I (Kim) remember occasions when Tom was away and I would have to get myself and three young children ready for church. Invariably, I would spend the church service in the nursery or managing the children and return home worn out, feeling I'd not worshipped at all. When I remarked to Marilynn that it didn't seem worth it, she reminded me that the point was not what I received from worship that day, but that I was establishing a pattern for my children and modeling that church was important, regardless of how I felt on a particular day or how much trouble it was to get there.

3. The Church Is to Serve

Christ commanded us to love God and to love our neighbor, and there's no better way to demonstrate our love than when we serve. Every Christian should be service-oriented. We take our cue from Christ who "made Himself of no reputation, taking the form of a bondservant, and coming in the likeness of men. And being found in appearance as a man, He humbled Himself and became obedient to the point of death, even the death of the cross" (Philippians 2:7–8 NKJV). A servant serves, and Christ served the God who sent Him to earth to redeem a lost world (John 5:30; 14:10).

Have you ever made food to take to the family whose mother was ill? Have you ever cleaned up your neighbor's trash that was scattered about by animals? Have you ever shoveled snow off someone's walk simply because you were physically able to do so? How about babysitting children for a couple who has not gone out for an evening alone in months or years? How about helping someone move who can't afford a moving company? Have you taken groceries to an elderly person on limited income? Can you create a shoe box of goodies and supplies to send to needy people overseas? Make sandwiches to hand out to street people? Save clothes to give to ministries catering to the needy? Have you thought of manning a Salvation Army collection kettle at Christmastime? All of these things can be done as a family. They are things that demonstrate our servant hearts, things done without any expectation of remuneration, gratitude, or reward.

There are other more substantial ways of serving people, such as caring for a family whose husband is incarcerated, or taking in at Christmas or Thanksgiving foreign students who have nowhere to go. Sometimes service can be walking with a single mother who is having trouble raising her children. This is something the whole family can share in as you open your lives and your home to serve others.

My (Tom) friend Dean Black is a certified mechanic who gets great joy out of donating his time after hours to fix the cars of people on limited income, charging them only for the cost of parts. I've been with him many times when he has received a phone call from a desperate person needing his advice. One of his paying customers decided to sell his car rather than repair it, so Dean bought it from him, fixed the car on his own time, and gave it to a church family in desperate need. To this family, Dean is an answer to their prayers.

Sadly, many people haven't appreciated serving others as a key aspect of Christlikeness. They live for themselves, their vacations, acquiring more stuff, and pleasures to gratify themselves. They seem oblivious to all those around them who are struggling daily to put food on the table, pay for housing, and to care for their health. Service shows our gratitude to God for all that He has given us physically, spiritually, socially, etc., and demonstrates to others our love for them and for God at the same time. This is a significant part of the Christian life that is best learned at an early age.

4. The Church Is to Help Christians Grow in Their Faith

Christ commanded us to "make disciples," teaching them to follow all that He commanded (Matthew 28:18–20). Reading Bible stories; posting Scripture memory verses; discussing the Sunday sermon on the way home from church; and asking about what they learned in Sunday School, home group, or Bible study are great ways to ensure our kids grow in their faith. We also pray with our children about the coming week and assure them God will guide them through the tough situations they face.

The church can only supplement or reinforce what parents are doing at home to help their children grow spiritually. Far too many parents have all but abandoned their God-given responsibility for their children's spiritual growth. Some believe making sure their kids go to Sunday School, kids club, or Bible study group is the extent of their duty. This couldn't be farther from the truth.

Rick Osborne, Christian author of more than 40 books on children and parenting, says:

> Current statistics show that well over 70 percent of children who are raised in the church leave the church after graduation. Why? There are a number of different factors, but most agree that probably the number one reason is that most Christian kids never mature in their knowledge and experience of the faith. If we taught our children math and science in the same haphazard way we teach them about their faith, not one of them would graduate.

These statistics are a wake-up call to parents to take charge of their children's spiritual growth, finding out what they believe about God and His church, and helping them to know how to live out their faith in a real world. This is something parents and churches can work on together to help our children stand firm in their faith.

Many parents feel inadequate to teach their children about spiritual things. A healthy church will equip parents! A good place to begin is sharing what God is teaching you each day so your children can grow with you as *you* grow in the Lord. Children learn more from *watching* than simply *listening*. As parents *demonstrate* their faith—as you openly *pray* to God; as you openly *study* His Word; as you *serve* others; and as you open your home for Bible studies, youth activities, and church events—children see devotion to God and His people and this cements parents' influence.

5. The Church Is to Be on Mission with God

The Apostle Paul writes: "For 'whoever calls on the name of the Lord shall be saved.' How then shall they call on Him in whom they have not believed? And how shall they believe in Him of whom they have not heard? And how shall they hear without a preacher? And how shall they preach unless they are sent? As it is written: 'How beautiful are the feet of those who preach the gospel of peace, Who bring glad tidings of good things!'" (Romans 10:13–15 NKJV).

There are a lot of people who think this is speaking to preachers and missionaries, but there were not many of these types of people when Paul wrote this. He was writing to believers meeting in those house churches in Rome. It was up to each person to be light in a dark world. Each church member was to let his "light so shine before men, that they may see your good works and glorify your Father in heaven" (Matthew 5:16 NKJV). This is the essence and goal of being on *mission* as a family—simply sharing God's love with those around us, serving others in the name of Jesus, and being a family of influence wherever God has placed us.

> OUR FAMILY BEGAN TO NOTICE THE TEENAGERS WHO LIKED TO HANG OUT AT OUR HOME. MOST OF THEM HAD VERY LITTLE RELIGIOUS OR CHURCH BACKGROUND, BUT THEY ENJOYED BEING IN OUR HOME.

It means being alert to the activity of God around your family and recognizing God's invitation to become involved in what He is doing. Our family began to notice the teenagers who liked to hang out at our home. Most of them had very little religious or church background, but they enjoyed being in our home and found it welcoming and inviting. They'd comment on the "fancy dinners" we served. My wife marveled that they would consider a meal of meat loaf a fancy dinner until she realized it wasn't the menu they meant—it was the experience of a family that all sat down to eat a home-cooked meal together with a table properly set!

They would comment on the "strange" relationship that existed between our children because our kids actually *liked* spending time with each other! They didn't see our children criticizing or arguing with each other or calling each other names. Our family was different and it intrigued them—because Christ is at the center.

We have come to realize that many teens don't have adults available to them after school or in the evenings to talk, to check up on them, to be interested in their lives. Their parents are working and busy with their own activities and assume their teens' growing independence means they don't need their parents' involvement to the same extent. We saw the teens coming to our home as an opportunity to listen to them, purposefully engage them in conversation, and seek to share the love of Christ with them. Sometimes God will bring the missions field right to your own doorstep!

I (Tom) recall my father once asking a church, "Do you believe God has a right to your life?" "Yes," they nodded. "Then do you believe God has the right to ask you to do whatever He chooses?" "Yes," they agreed. "Then do you accept that God has the right to ask you to go anywhere in the world at any time He chooses to?" "Yes," they responded, although not quite so exuberantly. "Then," he said, "how many of you have valid passports?" Only a few hands went up in the crowd. "Your lack of readiness to go says more about what you believe than your words do."

Passports can be obtained relatively quickly these days. But it is the heart that needs to be made ready first. One of Christ's last commandments is in Matthew 28:18–20 (NKJV):

And Jesus came and spoke to them, saying, "All authority has been given to Me in heaven and on earth. Go therefore and make disciples of all the nations, baptizing them in the name of the Father and of the Son and of the Holy Spirit, teaching them to observe all things that I have commanded you; and lo, I am with you always, even to the end of the age." Amen.

Here the command is not to *go*—that is assumed—but to *disciple, baptize,* and *teach* those who come to Christ through our witness. Christ assumes we'll want to share the great news of His love for people and how God sent His Son Jesus to die for people's sins and give them eternal life if they will believe in Him. The question is, in what capacity and to what destination will we go? As churches accept God's call on families' lives and His desire to use them significantly in His work to reach a lost world, they will begin to provide the resources families need to accomplish what God has called them to do. Further, they will surround families with love, support, and prayer daily for the work.

Many churches hold special ceremonies to send missionaries overseas to unreached people groups, but why not commission families as they go out to do what God has called them to do? Why not surround families with support, love, and prayer during a worship service, asking God's blessings, guidance, and power to be given them as they seek to be families of influence at their schools, on the sports field, at work, or as they go on their missions trips? Doing this demonstrates that families are an extension of the church into the community and are called, equipped, and used by God in exciting and creative ways. Paul puts *being on mission* in simple terms when he writes, "Therefore, as we have opportunity, let us do good to all, especially those of the household of faith" (Galatians 6:10 NKJV). □

STRENGTHENING FAMILIES

Martin Luther King Jr. once said, "Eleven o'clock Sunday morning is the most segregated hour of the week." In a way this is as true for the family. Sundays can be the most stressful, difficult, and divided day of the week in many homes. Many families arrive at church on Sunday morning and the teenager runs off to the youth building, the children head to their department, the mother heads to the women's class, the husband goes to the men's class, and they may never get back together until they meet at the car to leave for home. Often they have arrived in separate cars to begin with! Despite the fact that many churches offer numerous and varied activities for family members, little is done to actually encourage family life.

Churches today are adept at planning youth activities, children's church, Vacation Bible School, women's Bible studies, and men's outreach activities. These programs are great for discipling and spiritual growth. There is, though, an obvious void when we look for churches that are helping families become stronger and more intentional in their ministry. Where are the activities that build unity in the family or help parents talk with teenagers, or that offer to help families serve together? We can have great revivals and times of spiritual renewal, but we also need parent forums to provide encouragement to frustrated moms and dads, to give them scriptural and spiritual guidelines for raising their kids in the Lord. It's hard enough as it is to get our teenagers to talk with us during the week, but sending them off on Sundays to separate buildings with separate worship and separate Bible studies that promote separate social activities will not address this problem.

There are glimmers of hope, however. We see family camps and mother-and-daughter retreats. We see father-and-son breakfasts and family fall festivals. When families seem to be under attack from every angle, more can be done to encourage families to grow together: a family fun night, a family bowling night, a barbecue and church picnic with family activities, or even Bible quiz nights for the family. We also need churches that will design activities and programs to encourage families to serve together.

■ **FAITH COMMUNITY CHURCH** organized a churchwide Secret Valentine event where every person's name was put into a box and they, in turn, drew out someone's name to bless the week prior to Valentine's Day. Richard, a college student, drew the name of a widow well into her 80s and living in a nursing home. During the week preceding Valentine's, he secretly left her flowers and various notes and treats. When she learned Richard was her secret Valentine at the church social, she was so delighted that she became Richard's avid supporter and prayer partner. Richard continued to visit her in the nursing home for quite some time and she in turn prayed regularly for him. Though he did not seek anything in return, she slipped him money for books and tuition as she was able.

■ **NORTH SEA BAPTIST CHURCH** provides a night of activities designed to allow every member of the family to participate (except babies!): balloon volleyball in the auditorium, Ping-Pong blow ball in the foyer, indoor soccer in the fellowship hall, relay races, and scavenger hunts around the property. Each of the deacons/elders acts as a team leader and is given a portion of the church membership list to enlist teams. Name tags are made, team banners designed, and prizes awarded at the end for the teams with the most points. Dads and daughters hit balloons together, mothers and sons try to blow the Ping-Pong ball across the table without losing their chewing gum, teenagers drip with sweat as they try to score a goal on the deacon chairman guarding the soccer net—what a blast! More people come to these events than any other event hosted by the church all year! Why? Because families are desperate for something they can do together in a healthy and encouraging environment.

Many churches who can afford it have opted for building recreation centers, family activity facilities that house gyms, weight rooms, banquet halls, bowling alleys, game rooms, and more in an attempt to provide their people with meaningful family activities. But this is not possible for the vast majority of churches, so they have to be much more creative and intentional in their planning for families.

- David Fresch, a youth pastor, plans weekend retreats for mothers and daughters to come together overnight away from the busyness of their home life. Devotions are prepared and delivered by both mothers and daughters, a Bible study is provided by the pastor for them to work through together, and times of information sharing are planned throughout the weekend to promote intimacy and communication. This provides moms with an opportunity to talk with their daughters and get to know them on a deeper, different level. For some moms and daughters, it is a highlight of the year and a chance to build memories that will last a lifetime. For others not used to sharing at such a personal level, this can at first feel threatening or uncomfortable; but it is so important to have such times of personal discussion and communication on spiritual topics so that families can seek the Lord and grow together.

Some churches plan weekend campouts for young couples with their small children, for fathers and sons, or for entire families. Basic skills in starting campfires, cooking outdoors, setting up tents, fishing, and more are demonstrated, but more importantly, families grow together by joining in singing worship songs, having family devotions led by the dads, and by having fun together. It is the together part that is missing in so much of our lives as families.

Mark Holmen describes for churches and pastors what it looks like to support families in his book *Building Faith at Home: Why Faith at Home Must Be Your Church's #1 Priority*:

- Your men's and women's ministries equip men and women to live out their faith at home.
- Your small-group ministry focuses on equipping people and holds them accountable for living out their faith in their homes.

- Your prayer ministry equips every family to pray daily in their homes instead of focusing on a few big prayer events at the church.
- Your sermons include an emphasis on taking the message home and living it out on a daily basis.
- Your church's Bible studies equip adults to be like Christ in their homes, community, and world.
- Your children's ministry helps equip parents to talk with their children about faith.
- Your youth ministry helps parents keep their teenagers engaged in a walk with the Lord through ongoing faith talk in the home.
- Your outreach ministry would refocus what it does so that families could become involved in outreach as a family.
- Your preaching and teaching would provide more practical examples and personal challenges for Christlike living in the home. Fill-in-the-blank sermon notes would be changed to include a "Take It Home" section filled with questions to consider, application ideas to implement and additional Scriptures to study.

When churches begin to see families as powerhouses of God's activity, they will be more vigilant in helping them grow and lay strong foundations of faith in their homes. Churches that value and encourage their families will have limitless resources and opportunities for influencing their communities and their world for Christ.

Pastor Bruce Milne writes, in *Dynamic Diversity: Bridging Class, Age, Race and Gender in the Church*, "I have a dream of a Christian community where children, youth, middle-aged and seniors, boomers, busters, gen-Xers and millennials learn to respect and love and discover their profound need for each other; where people from all wealth and power backgrounds can live and relate and laugh together.

"I have a dream of a family where singles and married couples, and married couples with families, and single parents and divorcees are all affirmed in their worth before God and his people; a family where poor and rich, sophisticated and unsophisticated, the physically and mentally strong and the physically and mentally challenged have learned to walk together in love, and to appreciate and affirm each other." Amen. □

FAMILY-TIME REFLECTIONS

1. How would you rate the extent to which your church feels like a family?

2. What can you and your family do to encourage the family life of the church body?

3. Who in your church seems to be "on the outside" or disconnected with the body? If God has brought that individual to your attention, what will your response be to this as an invitation to welcome that individual inside the family?

4. What is your attitude toward visitors? Would they see your church as immediately welcoming and friendly, or cold and judgmental?

5. What do you do personally to help new people fit into their new spiritual home? Do you visit them at their home to see if they have any questions about their new community or the church? Do you learn about their background and spiritual gifts in order to help them serve God where He has brought them?

■ ■ ■

■ ■ ■

He who dwells in the shelter of the

Most High will rest in the shadow of

the Almighty. I will say of the LORD,

"He is my refuge and my fortress, my

God, in whom I trust"

(Psalm 91:1–2 KJV).

■ ■ ■

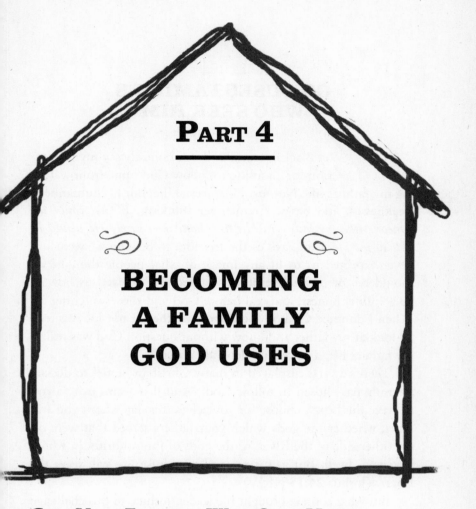

PART 4

BECOMING A FAMILY GOD USES

GOD USES FAMILIES WHO SEEK HIM
GOD USES FAMILIES WHO SERVE HIM
GOD REDEEMS AND USES TROUBLED FAMILIES
FAMILY-TIME REFLECTIONS
    STRATEGIES, ACTIVITIES, AND EXERCISES

GOD USES FAMILIES
WHO SEEK HIM

*M*el Blackaby recalls: "I can honestly say my inspiration for choosing to follow God came from watching my father's life. Not just his spiritual life, but his humanness, weaknesses, and flaws. I remember thinking, *If God could use someone like my father in His kingdom, then surely He would be able to use me.* Dad gave us the freedom to be who we were and never expected us to fit any image of what people thought we should be, or to act like others wanted. He showed us how to be genuine, honest, and real before God and those watching us. When I doubted God or questioned whether or not He was real, I'd look at my father and know without question God was real in my father's life, and I could depend on that."

There's a verse displayed in many Christian homes to declare a family has chosen to follow God: "And if it seems evil to you to serve the LORD, choose for yourselves this day whom you will serve, whether the gods which your fathers served that were on the other side of the River, or the gods of the Amorites in whose land you dwell. But as for me and my house, we will serve the LORD" (Joshua 24:15 NKJV).

But what context brought the leader, Joshua, to this challenge and choice? He was probably the oldest person alive in the Israelite camp. All of his generation, except Caleb's and Moses's families, had died in the wilderness because of their sin and rebellion against God. Joshua had been enslaved in Egypt and now, as a free man, stood in the Promised Land. He'd seen many battles, many miracles as God provided for their needs and safety faithfully, and the results of sin and rebellion and obedience and trust in God. The statement he makes is based on a lifetime of walking with God. He challenges the multitude to choose finally whom they will serve.

They respond with resounding affirmations of their dedication to God, "We also will serve the LORD, for He is our God" (Joshua 24:18 NKJV). But Joshua knows them. He knows about empty promises people can make. So he responds, "Now therefore...put away the foreign gods which are among you, and incline your heart to the LORD God of Israel" (Joshua 24:23 NKJV). The people were saying they would serve God only while they still had idols at home on their shelves! Their *words* sounded great, but their *actions* betrayed them. To their credit, they followed Joshua's instructions and remained faithful to God, at least as long as Joshua was alive.

As Christian parents, we know we too must put away that which is inconsistent with the Christian life and incline our heart to the Lord. We will pay a price for saying one thing in public and doing another in our home. Children are very keen observers; they see and point out inconsistencies. The way we live leaves big footprints for our children to follow, so we need to be sure we're leading in the right direction!

Our actions often have an immediate impact on our children following in our footsteps, but other times the results of our behaviors will not become known for years. Nevertheless, where we go, what we say, and what we do will shape and mold our children's thoughts, actions, and words.

The adage that our actions speak louder than our words is true. If our desire is for our children to have great communication with their spouses, to have servant hearts in their home, to be generous and caring toward others, to be willing to serve the Lord in whatever He asks of them, then we first need to model all of this in our own life. Knowing it's our responsibility to raise, train, disciple, and prepare our children for life with God means we take every opportunity to introduce them to God's ways and His purposes for them and help them to grow spiritually.

We need to ask ourselves, "If someone were to ask our children what we believe about God, what would they say? Would they be able to define such words as *prayer*, *faith*, *trust*, or *giving* based solely on what they observe? What do our lives say about who we believe God to be?"

When children are young in the faith or young in years, we must take time to explain to them why we go to church, sing songs of praise and worship, tithe, help others, and give to missions. Our children see us in our everyday lives; but do they see God as real, present, and integral to every area of our life?

Gaby Spicer says, "We do several things to establish God as the center of our home, and to help our children understand their role in the kingdom. We have a heart to serve the body, and to have our kids by our side as we do. We use service as a tool in discipling and helping them understand what it means to help, give, encourage, bless, and provide for those around us that have lack. We also show our kids they're important to us; we love them; and we are there to serve, encourage, bless, and provide for them. We believe that our family is our first responsibility; it is where we learn what it truly means to love."

Demonstrating Devotion to God

Parents' lives must demonstrate that developing a relationship with God is worth the time. Children need to see us spending time in God's Word and in prayer, in order to develop their quiet times with God. Keeping a devotional journal is worthwhile for us and giving it to our children later as a legacy of faith provides something valuable for them to read and understand more about our walk with God and our spiritual journey. We should be regularly sharing with our children what God is showing us in our devotional times with Him. They need to see us growing in our faith, knowledge of God, practice of Christian principles, worship, and in our love for God. They will carry their memories of parents with them forever.

Over the years, my (Tom) father, as a gesture to each of his five children, has given each a very used and worn Bible of his. As he begins studying in a new Bible, usually one with wider margins, he notes thoughts God shows him in his study time. We can read through them and not only get some good sermon or Bible study ideas but also see how God spoke to him through His Word.

My mother's grandmother, Great-Grandma Rooker, was a saintly woman. I only remember her as a frail, white-haired widow with a kind smile and a walker. She seemed ancient to me when I was a young child. It's strange to think now of the impact her life had on our family. After her husband died, she was left to raise her four children on her own. My grandmother, Carrie, was the oldest and had to go to work at a young age to help support the family.

Every Sunday, Great-Grandma dressed her children up in their Sunday-best clothes and went to church. Even on her meager income, she never failed to tithe, and taught her children to thank God even for what He was yet to provide. On more than one occasion, they sat down for a meal with nothing on the table and thanked God for what He was going to provide them. Sure enough, someone would drop off some food at their door to see them through. These stories of faithfulness, gratitude to God, and trust were passed down through the generations and serve as a challenge to our family to never doubt God's love for His people.

Devotion to God can also be demonstrated by being devoted to fellow Christians.

> If someone says, "I love God," and hates his brother, he is a liar; for he who does not love his brother whom he has seen, how can he love God whom he has not seen? And this commandment we have from Him: that he who loves God must love his brother also (1 John 4:20–21 NKJV).

Be careful of criticisms about other Christians, observations of church inadequacies, and discontent with how things are done at church. All leave impressions on children who may not be able to understand that we can still love people while disagreeing with them. Helping our children have a healthy understanding of God's people and His church means helping them understand that church is more than a building, activities, and a place to meet with God; it's a place where we gather together as God's family, warts and all!

Some parents will need to apologize to their children for how they've spoken harshly against the pastor or other church members. Little ears overhear phone conversations and car talk and little hearts and minds can be needlessly filled with second-hand resentments and denigrating thoughts against church family members who really do love them. Wise parents will use every opportunity to help their children love their church family and appreciate all that God has done for them.

Demonstrating a Desire to Grow

Growth implies change: in our attitudes, character, disciplines, and choices. Desiring to grow means we'll continually place ourselves where we will be challenged spiritually such as Bible studies, home groups, and accountability groups. Maintaining our spiritual status quo will not be acceptable—we'll desire to go deeper with God. (See Hebrews 5:12–14).

Growing means acknowledging when we have sinned and asking forgiveness of God and of others. It means facing the reality of who we are and allowing God access to our lives to mold and shape as He sees fit. It means responding to God's truth as He reveals it to us with faith *and* action. Do our children see this process being worked out in our lives? Do we share with our children God's work in our lives (as appropriate)?

As a young woman, I (Kim) would not have described myself as an angry person. I wasn't negative and contentious or prone to outbursts. I saw myself as pleasant, loving, and agreeable. However, when I found myself at home day after day raising two small children, I became irritable, impatient, harsh, critical, and prone to yelling and even angry outbursts. I didn't like the person I saw emerging and realized my perfectionism was manifesting itself in ungodly ways. This was not the character of Christ I professed to be seeking. I began to pray and memorize Scriptures that spoke about the character I longed to see displayed in my life.

I soon realized I was unable to change significantly on my own strength and that I needed to depend on God and His Holy Spirit to work out of my life negative and damaging traits and work into my life the fruit of the Spirit. Over time, I began to see a change. I would repeat those verses to myself and pray when I was becoming impatient or irritable. I'd still find myself yelling or speaking harshly on occasion, but those occasions were becoming less frequent and I apologized and prayed with my kids when they did occur. They saw that their mom was seeking God and trying to change, admitting when she had sinned and seeking forgiveness. My children are teenagers now, but I can still point to the page of "anger" verses in my journal from that time and can talk about how God changed this angry mom into the one they see today.

Mel Blackaby says, "Dad never told us what to do when we came to him with problems. Instead he told us to seek the Lord and would almost always ask us, 'What is God saying to you?'"

Demonstrating Dependence on God

Depending on God should be a lifestyle rather than an emergency response relegating God to the spiritual realm and leaving Him out of the practical aspects of daily life. God spent 40 years teaching the people of Israel to depend on Him for guidance, strength, protection, and daily provisions of food—all the necessities of life. Our children need to understand how dependent we are on God for our health, safety, livelihood, and homes. Cancer, economic downturn, tornadoes, fire, car accidents, and war can change everything in a blink of an eye. But we know that our lives are in His hands.

> Trust in Jehovah with all thy heart, and lean not upon thine own understanding: in all thy ways acknowledge him, and he will direct thy paths (Proverbs 3:5–6 ASV).

Our children learn dependence on God as they watch us depend on Him and see God provide; as they see us pray before major decisions, seek His guidance in situations, search His Word for answers, and pray before panicking when a crisis arises.

Some years ago, I was traveling with Kim and our family, sightseeing near Rimini, Italy, on a Sunday afternoon. Suddenly, dashboard lights lit warnings and the brakes, air-conditioning, and steering failed. I asked my family to pray for us to find a gas station. One appeared right away on our side of the road—though it was closed. Again, we prayed for God's help. Within minutes the station owner and his daughter arrived and found a tow truck, who drove us to the only mechanic open that day. When the mechanic said, "We have no such part in all of Italy!" we breathed a short prayer of desperation. A part was found (literally across the street from the mechanic) and we were on the road to a family conference, on schedule.

When I shared the story at the conference, a man responded, "Tom, just about the same thing happened to my family on the way here; but I have to admit, rather than asking my family to pray, they heard some pretty foul language come out of my mouth when the car broke down. I am ashamed of what my kids learned about me from how I handled that crisis." It is my desire that our children will learn by watching their parents turn to God in times of crisis.

GOD USES FAMILIES WHO SERVE HIM

Demonstrating a Servant Heart

*J*esus said, "My Father has been working until now, and I have been working" (John 5:17 NKJV). This hasn't changed today, except now the Father and the Son *and* the Spirit are all working together in the hearts of people all around us. It's our turn to say, "Our Lord has been working until now, and our family is also working." Many times serving Christ is *hard* work! More often, serving God is a joy, privilege, honor, and can be a lot of fun. But serving God is always rewarding. Serving God together as a family results in deeper relationships between members, us and the Lord, and us and those to whom we minister with God's help.

I learned a lot from watching my father pastor over the years. Growing up in the Blackaby household meant not having a father around very much. He taught day and evening classes at our Bible school and had meetings and Bible studies to lead. Every Sunday afternoon and Tuesday night, for several years, he drove 90 miles north of home to preach at a small mission church in Prince Albert, Saskatchewan. Sometimes we would stop at the last gas station on the edge of town and pick up a coffee and a warm cinnamon bun for the road. These drives were times we could spend with our father and meet with believers who wanted to study the Word of God but had no one to teach them. After two and a half years, a mission pastor was called and the trips stopped, but a mark had been left on my life.

A few years later as a teenager, I began to travel to a nearby town once a week to lead a Bible study with the youth at Colonsay, one of our mission points. On many a cold winter's night, several of us youth would pile into our family station wagon and drive ourselves 40 miles to lead games and a Bible study with a group of teenagers who had no church of their own to attend. Even as high school students, sacrificing to be on mission was simply what we did.

Some 35 years later, I found myself boarding an airplane every Tuesday morning to fly 40 minutes to another city to lead a mission Bible study and return home alone late at night. This continued for well over a year until a mission pastor was called and a church established. My father instilled in me a desire to help people know God—not by his teaching, but by his example. I realized that someone had to invest time, energy, and resources for people to have the Scriptures taught where there was no church for them to attend. My father demonstrated his willingness to serve and I saw the fruit of his labor grow into a full-fledged church that in time started several mission churches on its own.

Demonstrating a Willingness
to Say Yes to God's Invitations

A heart ready to serve God will respond when He calls. A family seeking after God will recognize opportunities He puts in their path as His invitation to join Him in what He is about to do. Not every opportunity is an invitation from God, but through prayerful consideration God will reveal His will each time.

God allowed Mordecai and Esther a unique opportunity to be a family of influence. Mordecai had adopted his uncle's child, Esther, and was raising her as his own daughter. Mordecai was both her legal guardian and her trusted advisor. He was a godly man who worshipped the Lord God and who had raised Esther in the fear of the Lord. This unlikely duo was called upon by God-engineered circumstances to put their lives on the line in order to avert the massacre of God's people.

From orphan to queen of Persia, God chose to use a family thrown together by tragic circumstances to save His people from annihilation. This family was used by God because they worshipped and honored God, recognized His activity in their lives, and responded with faith to His invitation to be involved in His saving work.

When my (Tom) maternal grandfather Melvin Wells told his family they were moving from Oklahoma to California in the 1940s, he explained God was calling them to go as missionaries to a small denomination of churches that desired to make a large impact. They joined a small struggling church in Riverside and immediately became integrally involved. Every Thursday night the whole family dressed up and followed up with those who had come to visit their church the previous Sunday.

My grandmother Carrie led the girls' missions group at the church and began instilling in the minds of her daughters and the other children the importance of missions. After Grandfather retired from Sears and Roebuck, he and Carrie volunteered with the Foreign Mission Board (now International Mission Board) to go to Zambia to govern a missionary children's home and to direct the Bible Way Correspondence program. I remember as a child receiving blue aerogram letters with the strangest stamps on them from M. A. Wells. Occasionally we would get a cassette tape of them sending greetings to us from Africa.

Not only did my grandparents teach about missions, they lived it. This had a big influence on my parents. When I was about eight years old, my parents sensed a call to missions and intended to take us all to Africa where they would serve as missionaries. But God redirected us to Canada in 1970 where my father would discover the lessons that comprised his book, *Experiencing God: Knowing and Doing the Will of God.*

Knowing how my mother was raised to be missions-minded and service-oriented, it was not surprising when she decided to take our family to a native Indian reserve near Cochin, Saskatchewan, to conduct Vacation Bible School for local children two weeks one summer. We brought craft supplies, found picnic tables, pumped up soccer balls, and prepared lessons for each day. Our accommodation was a couple of tents and our prayer was that it would not rain! I don't remember a lot of other details, but the fact that we went to serve people we did not know in an unfamiliar place, not knowing exactly what we were going to face when we got there, impressed me.

Demonstrating an Eternal Focus

We prepare our children not simply for life on their own but for eternity. All of our thoughts, plans, and actions should reflect that we're integrally connected to the eternal kingdom of God. This will help us better prioritize how we spend time, money, and how we plan our activities. We want to have immediate, long-term, and eternal influence on our children.

Such things as showing respect for others, having personal discipline to clean their rooms, do their homework, and giving their best effort in sports and other interests are important now. Long term, we desire to see our children faithfully carrying out responsibilities, standing firm in the midst of trials, not giving in to peer pressure, and regularly attending church. Finally, choices that will have an eternal impact on their life include a habit of personal devotional time with God, sharing their faith with others, investing in God's kingdom, supporting missionaries and ministries, and having a strong prayer life.

Some time ago, Kim and I had to curtail our high school daughter's increasing reclusiveness—in her room with her computer. We were not happy with her spending so much time away from the rest of the family. We suggested to her that we could unplug the wireless modem if her computer time became more important to her than spending time with her family. Thankfully her protests were modified by her understanding that we valued her presence and her relationship with us and her two brothers. My daughter appreciated that even though her parents seemed stricter than others, they actually cared to have her around and valued her as an important part of the family.

Cris Rowan, a pediatric occupational therapist and sensory specialist in Sechelt, British Columbia, urges parents to bond with their children at an early age or risk seeing them turn into Internet addicts by the time they become teenagers. "Children are disconnecting from themselves, from others, from nature, and that disconnect...is resulting in what I can only describe as the perfect storm."

Richard Blackaby writes, "We tried to involve our kids whenever we could; for example, taking them with me when I ministered in the nursing home. Now that they are older, I take them with me on international trips and have them share something. I was able to take one son with me and Dad to the Philippines where we met the president. He had to miss a week of school, but I thought that would be life-changing. I provided opportunities for my kids to be around strong Christians to let them see first-hand what a dynamic Christian looks like. When the kids take on leadership tasks, like preaching on Youth Sunday at our church, I give constructive, encouraging feedback. I encourage our kids to take leadership roles when it is suitable for them. I always try and debrief with them afterward to help them learn from what they are doing." □

GOD REDEEMS AND USES
TROUBLED FAMILIES

*I*t's safe to say families face today face a multitude of problems, some due to poor choices family members have made. Smothering debt, addictions, affairs, violence in the home, deceit, gambling, workaholism, abandonment, and divorce are a few of the challenges families face. Do these challenges mean God can't redeem and use a family with these or other issues? Of course not. When we bring to Him all we have to offer, He'll show us how to use who we are, what we've experienced, and all that we have to further His kingdom and glorify His name. God is able and willing to use any type of family that seeks to serve Him.

A Divided Home

Many families have only one Christian parent and an unbelieving parent, which poses real challenges to serving the Lord as a family. Home is divided in focus, direction, and values. Acts 16 describes Paul's journey to Derbe and Lystra where he came to know a young disciple named Timothy. Apparently his father was not a believer, while his mother and grandmother demonstrated a deep faith in Christ. A home divided by culture and religion still produced a co-worker with the Apostle Paul (Acts 17:14) and a young pastor for the early churches described in Acts and Paul's epistles (1 Thessalonians 3:2, 6; Philippians 2:19–23). We're never told that Timothy's dad ever came to Christ or ever accepted his son's devotion to God. But we do know God chose to use a young man who came from a challenging home life. Paul wrote to Timothy describing his heritage of faith and encouraging him to stay strong in his commitment to Christ (2 Timothy 1:1–5 NKJV).

Regardless of the circumstances in which your family has come together, when you honor God in your home, it can be a powerful instrument in His hands to impact your community. For example, a woman named Margery wanted to support our dad's church, but her husband was not a believer and refused to allow her to give any monetary gifts to the church. However, she had two children who were always dressed in the best quality clothing. She knew our family had four boys, all of whom were younger than her son. She sensed that she could minister to the pastor's family by giving us her son's slightly worn clothing. Every couple of months we would receive a box of clothes that her son had "outgrown." Our mother had to buy few clothes for us while we remained in that church. Margery also was a great cook and always brought lots of baked offerings to church events to share. She found ways to encourage her church family while trying to honor her husband's wishes.

Single Parents

Most single parents we know didn't plan to be single. Whether it was a teenage pregnancy, divorce, separation, a spouse's death, or issues of safety, they find themselves trying to be both Mom and Dad to their children. Single parents carry the whole load of parenting on their own shoulders, but God notices. And God steps in.

A single mother, Hagar, and her son Ishmael faced a tragic situation in the Old Testament but God intervened. Abraham's lack of faith led him to bear a child through Sarah's servant Hagar. Sarah eventually became jealous (Genesis 21) and threw out Hagar and Ishmael to wander alone and unprotected in the desert. Hagar could not bear to watch her son die and cried to God for help. He heard her cry and said, "Get up, go and pick him up, and comfort him. I will make a great nation out of his descendants" (Genesis 21:18 GNT). God provided a spring of water for them, saving their lives.

God knows the anxieties single parents face and the sacrifices they make for their children. Men or women abandoned by their spouses, rejected by those who are unwilling to parent, or subjected to abuse can have God's Spirit as parent in the home. God is there when a single parent is stretched beyond limits. And He can take a son abandoned by his father or a daughter abandoned by her mother and make those children a great blessing to others. God delights in doing so.

Take the testimony of Robert, whose wife left him. Robert raised their three young children, remained devoted to God, worked hard, and had positive relationships. Though Rick walked a lonely road and had many questions for God, he was faithful and lived with integrity before his kids and others.

Years later, God brought into Robert's life a godly wife with a servant heart. Together they minister to families. God continues to use him as an encouragement to others and as witness to His faithful goodness in the midst of trials and testing.

But what about divorce? Nearly half of all marriages in the Western world end in divorce today. God hates divorce, right? Yes (Malachi 2:16), and He is grieved over the scars and trauma it causes families. He also deeply loves people and is able, over time, to work through the mistakes people make or the trauma that one parent inflicts on his or her family, to bring healing. We should never gloss over people's sin, but when God sees a repentant heart, He provides forgiveness and restoration of relationships.

Families Hoping for a Fresh Start

Perhaps you're a parent who wants God to use your family, but you realize you and your children or spouse have been drifting apart, and you don't know how to come back together. Maybe your children now have their own friends and separate interests, and lines of communication have not been kept up for whatever reason. You're not sure where to start to bring your family back together so that God can use you in His kingdom. There's hope.

When the angel predicted John the Baptist's birth to his father Zechariah (Luke 1:17 GNT), one of John's ministries pertained to the family:

> He will go ahead of the Lord, strong and mighty like the prophet
> Elijah. He will bring fathers and children together again; he

will turn disobedient people back to the way of thinking of the righteous; he will get the Lord's people ready for him.

God can warm hearts that are cold toward one another and breathe new life into relationships. This begins with having a clean heart toward God. When *your* heart is surrendered to God, your heart will also turn back to your family. When *you* are filled with the Spirit of God, you will be at peace with your brother and sister, spouse, or child. One result of turning back to God is that God begins to work in relationships with others. Hearts that were once turned in different directions can now be aligned through God's Spirit and they can begin to work together.

Family members who were once distracted by worldly pursuits, selfish gain, personal gratification, self-centered ambitions, and indifference can now be united together through the Lord working in their hearts. If your family is divided and hearts are not turned toward God or toward one another, ask God's Spirit to perform a miracle in members' hearts and minds so that together you can serve the Lord as He intends.

Wounded Families Are Precious to God

What about an abusive parent or families whose kids are caught in drug abuse, sexual activity, gang culture? How can God use these families? From my experience, God can use anyone from any situation if they are willing to follow Him step-by-step and be obedient as He leads. And that is the key: following God.

We have friends serving the Lord who grew up in foster care. We know pastors and missionaries whose fathers were alcoholics, who were sexually abused, whose father left the home when the children were small, and whose mother abandoned the family. Some of God's best servants have been former gang members or terrorists, murderers, adulterers, liars, and thieves. But through God's grace and the work of the Holy Spirit, God has done a miracle in their hearts and continues to help them overcome their past, to bring healing to their emotional scars, and put their feet back on solid ground.

Two families in our church faced the trauma of adultery. The husband of one family with four children had an affair with the wife in another family of two children. They refused to break off their adulterous relationship, resulting in the devastation of two families, and traumatized the rest of the church. This was not a time for service projects or missions trips; this was a time for healing, prayer, counsel, and pastoral care for these two broken families. Both had been heavily involved in ministry in the church, serving on committees, teaching Sunday School, organizing events; but all of that stopped to allow them time to heal and deal with their pain and suffering caused by the sin of two selfish and sinful parents.

It has been some years now since that happened and one of the families has moved on and recovered to the point of once again being able to serve the Lord with gladness, though the scars remain. What was incredible to observe, however, was the godly response the wife of the adulterous husband demonstrated through it all. Her faith and devotion to God remained exemplary in the midst of incredible anguish and her four children gained newfound respect for her during this time as she began to raise them without the support or involvement of their father.

Families in the middle of trauma should focus first on working through their turmoil in the home rather than embarking on service. Often there remains bitterness, anger, resentment, hostility, and emotional (if not physical) scars after trauma occurs. Getting too involved in ministry or missions activity can actually mask the pain and prevent God from doing a mighty work of healing. His healing brings forgiveness, reconciliation, and peace back into a home. Some families need to focus on restoring unity in the home, or learn ways to serve God that will not cause further division or irritation in the home.

When a Family Comes to Christ Later in Life

In these instances of transformation, there's potential for serious problems. Patterns of worldliness and well-entrenched priorities of money and career must give way to Christian values and priorities. As this new Christian foundation begins in the home, there can be serious conflict with children who are not yet following their parent's or parents' new beliefs. Priorities begin to change in the home; money is now spent differently; and values shift from being self-centered to God-centered.

Some children will resist the changes and may even rebel openly. They wanted the newest TV instead of sending that money to support missionaries. They wanted to go out with their friends instead of helping out at the homeless shelter. They wanted to go shop in Paris this summer instead of on a missions trip to Central America. Their lives have been turned upside down because of their parents' newfound faith. It may take them a while to understand how deep the changes really are, and they may never really accept the new lifestyle or values and may challenge their parents' resolve regularly.

In this case, remember the Lord loves your children more than you do and pray regularly and fervently that God's Spirit will work in your children's hearts to bring them to Christ. Kids always watch to see if their parents' commitment to Christ is genuine. They want to see consistency between speech and actions. They need to see that their parents love them more now than ever before and continue to want God's best for them. Invite them to participate in various ministry opportunities along the way, but do not force them to be involved. With God's help, you will begin to see their hearts soften as the Spirit draws them with love into His kingdom.

Rebellious Children

There seems to be a prodigal in many Christian families and for various reasons. In Luke 15, Jesus provides us with the parable of the prodigal son. The overall theme of this parable is unconditional love of the father toward his children, even in the face of open rebellion and disregard.

Many fathers would have handled the return of the son very differently. Some would accuse, blame, curse, ridicule, mock, and shame the son. Others might demand recompense, reject the son, or give him the "I told you so" or the "Do you have any idea what you have done to our family?" speech. This father chooses to focus on his son's repentance and the exciting fact that he is alive after all he has been through. This story centers on the importance of forgiveness toward one's children and reminds us that we are to forgive as we have been forgiven. Not only that, but God will forgive us "just as we have forgiven those who have sinned against us" (Matthew 6:12 NLT).

In this parable, we learn how the children's choices can take them out of the blessings of a family as both the younger and older son were in jeopardy at some point. Even though each person in the home benefited from the father's faithfulness, each chose to respond differently and faced different results. What gives parents hope in this story is that even when a child strays from the family, God's Spirit is still active in the child's life, drawing the child back to Himself.

No parent is perfect, and sometimes God's Spirit needs to work as much in the hearts of the parents as He does in the heart of the wayward child. We can never forget how God works through a family's history and through prayer. Remember how God can use what a child has been taught earlier in his or her life and bring it back to remembrance. Under no circumstances should we ever give up on our children! We, too, can be parents who remain faithful to watch, pray, and rejoice as a family when a child gets on the right path.

Not all children will respond to God as we parents would like. Even children in godly homes will choose to rebel for a season of life and turn their backs on God and their family for various reasons. Phil Waldrep has a helpful book on this topic called *Parenting Prodigals: Six Principles for Bringing Your Son or Daughter Back to God.* This book gives parents hope and clear strategies to work toward redemption. As far as it depends on parents, we are responsible to raise our children in the "fear and admonition of the Lord"; but we are not responsible for the decisions or life choices of our adult children.

Can a family with a prodigal child serve God? Yes. We are still called to serve the Lord whether or not our children follow our example. As mentioned earlier, God may have some work to do in parents' hearts to enable them to serve Him better as they learn to love the prodigal child as He does.

Our friends John and Grace are determined to be a family God uses. Grace grew up in a family that loved and served God. Her parents were active in many areas of service in the church. Eventually, Grace became the church secretary and uses her gifts of organization and service to ensure that every church event is well planned and executed. Her husband, John, uses his skills at carpentry and masonry, designing and building the church baptistery, sets for musical events, and many other projects. Their daughter, Lauren, works with youth and in many other ministries of the church.

But their son, Chris, wandered from his relationship with God and the church in his youth. Grace and John determined to love their son and maintain a good relationship with him despite his life choices. When Chris married, they allowed him and his wife and daughter to move into the lower level of their home. Chris still was not walking with the Lord, but John and Grace kept the door open by not criticizing and nagging their son and began to build a relationship with their new daughter-in-law.

Soon Chris and his wife were attending church and coming to other church events. By maintaining a loving relationship with him, and living an authentic relationship with God before him, God has enabled John and Grace to begin to see their prodigal walking back home.

Christian parents are never alone in raising their children: "And if a man prevail against him that is alone, two shall withstand him; and a threefold cord is not quickly broken" (Ecclesiastes 4:12 ASV). Where one person may have trouble against an enemy, two persons can overcome the enemy, but three standing together can withstand anything that comes against them. In the home, where one parent will struggle at times, two parents are strong when they stand together and work together, but with the Lord as the third parental force in the home, they can overcome whatever obstacles they face.

Richard Blackaby writes, "The Christian life ought to be characterized by joy, and lots of it. We decided that if our teenagers were going to embrace our faith, it would have to be attractive. When Christian homes overflow with joy, then children are much less likely to experience rebellion. Why rebel against a place that brings you constant joy? So we sought to make our home a fun place and our faith a joyful one.

"We also sought to be honest with our kids to let them know when we were facing challenges and did so in a positive way. We made a point never to talk poorly about our church or its staff. We encouraged our kids to always look for the positive in everything, even if there were some negatives too. We sought to keep our faith 'real.' Not surprisingly, our kids and many of their friends who were in our home often saw that being a Christian really is the best way to live. Now they're all following the Lord on their own. And they know how to laugh and to enjoy life." ☐

> WE MADE A POINT NEVER TO TALK POORLY ABOUT OUR CHURCH OR ITS STAFF. WE ENCOURAGED OUR KIDS TO ALWAYS LOOK FOR THE POSITIVE IN EVERYTHING, EVEN IF THERE WERE SOME NEGATIVES TOO.

FAMILY-TIME REFLECTIONS

STRATEGIES, ACTIVITIES, AND EXERCISES

Prayer

The most effective tool parents have in their parenting "tool kit" is without any doubt prayer. Prayer reminds us that the "third parent," the Spirit of God, is active:

- When we're unable to be present with our teenagers at all times, the Lord is beside them.
- Where we cannot change the hearts and minds of our children, the Lord can.
- When we fail and let our children down, the Lord never fails, and never lets them down.
- He brings wisdom to every difficult situation.
- He reveals the truth of every murky circumstance.
- He can unite us together as families and help us serve in His strength.
- He watches over us in our homes while we're asleep.
- He takes care of our needs when we do not know where else to turn.
- He is dependable when everyone else fails us.

Even parents who are devoted Christians giving their best effort to raise their kids—reading all the latest parenting books and listening to all the greatest advice—will fail from time to time. But the Lord steps in to help us recover from stumbling and brings forgiveness and restoration in the family through His Spirit's presence in our homes. Prayer is the means by which hearts can be changed and relationships restored. Prayer is what brings the wayward child home, the wandering parent back, and heals the broken hearts, all things that only God can do.

Telling Stories

Stories are a powerful tool for teaching children because they're easily remembered and rehearsed with children. In fact, children often recall stories we've long forgotten because their imaginations were stimulated with mental pictures of things long past.

The genius of the people of Israel was their oral history. They had been nomadic wanderers, slaves in foreign lands, a people devastated time and again by invading armies, swept off to Babylon through forced migration, and intermarried with various other people groups. But they kept their identity because of their shared history passed down from generation to generation.

They would have heard the phrase "the God of Abraham, Isaac, and Jacob" repeatedly as children and listened to the stories of the Exodus with Moses, the flood with Noah, the big fish that swallowed Jonah, and Elijah calling fire down on Mount Carmel. These would have left vivid mental pictures in children's minds. And each time they were told with the tagline "and God was faithful to His promises" or "God defeated the enemies" or "God gave the victory," or something that would help their children know that they were special people because God had chosen them to be His prized possession.

> "Listen, my people, to my teaching, and pay attention to what I say. I am going to use wise sayings and explain mysteries from the past, things we have heard and known, things that our ancestors told us. We will not keep them from our children; we will tell the next generation about the LORD's power and his great deeds and the wonderful things he has done. He gave laws to the people of Israel and commandments to the descendants of Jacob. He instructed our ancestors to teach his laws to their children, so that the next generation might learn them and in turn should tell their children. In this way they also will put their trust in God and not forget what he has done, but always obey his commandments" (Psalm 78:1–7 GNT).

Telling stories is never an end in itself; there is a purpose: to build faith in succeeding generations. "In this way they also will put their trust in God...always obey his commandments." Although Grandpa Gerald Blackaby died before most of his grandchildren were born, we feel like we know him through the numerous stories we were told about his life and character. Stories of planting evangelical churches in remote communities; of refusing to compromise his principles in the face of possible retribution; of God's faithfulness to him as a soldier in World War I; of humor, wit, and community service; and stories that even today continue to influence generations that follow in his steps.

When our two teenagers returned from their missions trip to a Russian orphanage, they could not stop telling stories of their time there. That was their way of sharing their time in ministry. We could hear their emotional reactions to seeing the poverty, we could imagine the smells, we could imagine the sounds they heard, and we could imagine the wonderful things they had seen. But what we were impressed with most was how they grew in the Lord during their experience on mission.

Valuing Each Individual Member

Young and old, male or female, can live out and proclaim the gospel message. Ephesians 4:11–14 helps parents see that each family member is equipped in particular ways by Christ Himself in order to serve Him. Spiritual gifts are designed to be used for ministering to others, "to prepare all God's people for the work of Christian service, in order to build up the body of Christ" (v. 12 GNT). Children can share Bible stories with others, the basic truths of how to become a Christian, and pray for those in need. They can encourage, serve, pray, sing, help, and do many things appropriate to their age. They are part of Christ's body, the church, and will desire to help others and serve their Lord because of the influence of Christ in your home. When Peter preached in Jerusalem at Pentecost, he said,

This is what I will do in the last days, God says: "I will pour out my Spirit on everyone. Your sons and daughters will proclaim my message; your young men will see visions, and your old men will have dreams. Yes, even on my servants, both men and women, I will pour out my Spirit in those days, and they will proclaim my message" (Acts 2:17–18 GNT).

What an awesome responsibility and privilege we have been given from God! This verse should sensitize us to the fact that God may be at work in the life of one or more of our children, calling them to special service for Him. It is so exciting to see God's hand molding and shaping children and drawing them to know Him. This is our hope for every child.

The Apostle Paul wrote in Ephesians 2:10 (NKJV): "For we are his workmanship, created in Christ Jesus for good works, which God prepared beforehand, that we should walk in them." It's our belief that God has assignments for every family as they submit to His lordship and to His will for them. Christ spent much time in prayer with His Father seeking to know what His assignment was to be for the next day, and in His time with His Father, God revealed where it was that He was working.

Take time regularly with each of your children to ask them what God is doing in their hearts. Ask them if God is leading them in any particular direction or impressing certain things on their hearts. Clarify with your children what God may be saying to them, and it will help you know better how to pray for them in the days and years ahead.

Identifying Spiritual Markers

One of the exercises in Henry Blackaby's *Experiencing God: Knowing and Doing the Will of God,* is to look at the "spiritual markers" in our lives to help determine what God's will is. Spiritual markers identify times of transition, decision, or direction when one clearly knew God was guiding him or her. These markers may not come often, but they are significant points in our walk with God.

My father, Henry Blackaby, often tells the story of our family's move to Canada in 1970. Before we went to the church in Saskatoon, the church was so discouraged they intended to disband if he would not go as their pastor. When he eventually moved to Saskatoon as pastor, the chairman of the deacons left the church because he had hoped the church would be closed. Things were very difficult with less than a dozen people left. We worked hard visiting, witnessing, and everything we knew to do. We enlisted missions teams from America to come and help in the summers. After 3½ years, we had 30 in Sunday School! My older brother, Richard, said to our mom, "Mom, I feel so sorry for Dad. Dad preaches such good sermons and gives an invitation week after week, and nobody comes." So my mom told my dad that he needed to have a word with his son. Dad sat Richard down and said, "Richard, don't feel sorry for your dad. It is a great honor to be asked by God to represent Him, and it is more than I deserve and more than I am capable of handling. The Bible says, "He that goeth forth and weepeth, bearing precious seed, shall doubtless come again with rejoicing, bringing his sheaves with him" (Psalm 126:6 KJV). Dad said, "I don't know how long God wants to let us labor here with all of our heart, but I believe we're where He wants us to be. I'm going to pray that God will one day let you see the harvest." God did! Not many years after that his older three boys were all called into the ministry along with dozens of others that God would bring into our church in the next 12 years.

> FAMILIES CAN DO THIS SPIRITUAL MARKERS EXERCISE BY JOURNALING WHAT GOD HAS DONE IN THEIR LIVES UP TO THIS POINT, INCLUDING THE TOUGH TIMES AND THE GOOD, TRIALS AND THE VICTORIES, CHALLENGES AND THE SUCCESSES.

Families can do this spiritual markers exercise by journaling what God has done in their lives up to this point, including the tough times and the good, the trials and the victories, the challenges and the successes had together. When we're able to identify what God has done in our past, we can better understand exactly what God may be up to in the days ahead. Every struggle, victory, challenge, and success lined up and seen in context provides a better picture of where God is leading a family in ministry and community involvement.

Perhaps you've coached your children in a sport and moved up with them through the ranks as they grew. Now God shows you an opportunity to go on short-term missions overseas to lead a family sports camp. Your children can help guide other children as you coach. When we understand how God works in His people's lives, we realize He takes everything from our past and present and uses it to bring Himself glory in the future. ☐

■ ■ ■

Tell it to your children, and let your

children tell it to their children, and

their children to the next generation

(Joel 1:3).

■ ■ ■

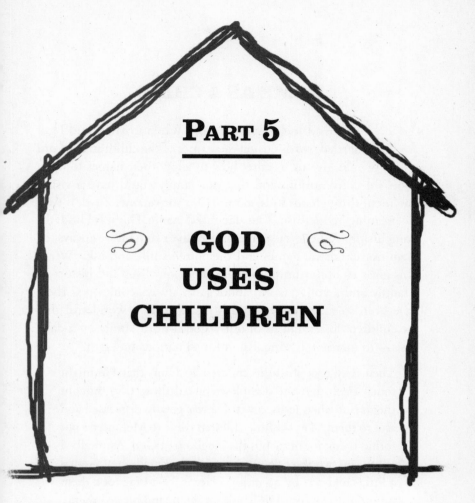

PART 5

GOD USES CHILDREN

COME AS A CHILD

Our friend Joel Vestal tells us, "When my wife and I got married, we discussed the names of the children the Lord would give us to raise, how to allow their names to open doors for conversation, and that our family could have a vision statement through our kids' names. Our son's name, Zayd, is Arabic meaning 'to increase.' Our daughter's name, Daya, is Hindi for 'compassion.' Whenever we meet an Arab or Indian, we always tell them our children's names and they often smile and ask, 'Why?' This gives us opportunity to share about our lives and history as a family and a conversation about faith always comes up. There have been so many conversations like this. It is wonderful that the children do remind us of our vision for our family on a daily basis—'to increase in compassion for all nations on earth.'"

> Then they brought little children to Him, that He might touch them; but the disciples rebuked those who brought them. But when Jesus saw it, He was greatly displeased and said to them, "Let the little children come to Me, and do not forbid them; for of such is the kingdom of God. Assuredly, I say to you, whoever does not receive the kingdom of God as a little child will by no means enter it." And He took them up in His arms, put His hands on them, and blessed them.
>
> Now as He was going out on the road, one came running, knelt before Him, and asked Him, "Good Teacher, what shall I do that I may inherit eternal life?" So Jesus said to him, "Why do you call Me good? No one is good but One, that is, God. You know the commandments: 'Do not commit adultery,' 'Do not murder,' 'Do not steal,' 'Do not bear false witness,' 'Do not defraud,' 'Honor your father and your mother.'" And he answered and said to Him, "Teacher, all these things I have kept from my youth."

Then Jesus, looking at him, loved him, and said to him, "One thing you lack: Go your way, sell whatever you have and give to the poor, and you will have treasure in heaven; and come, take up the cross, and follow Me." But he was sad at this word, and went away sorrowful, for he had great possessions. Then Jesus looked around and said to His disciples, "How hard it is for those who have riches to enter the kingdom of God!" (Mark 10:13–23 NKJV).

God includes every passage in the Bible for a reason. Matthew 19, Mark 10, and Luke 18 all contain versions of this event in their Gospel accounts of Christ's life on earth. During His ministry, every type of person came to Him: rich people, religious leaders, the poor, crippled, blind, women caught in adultery, women with broken marriages, businessmen, rulers, soldiers, and more. But in this passage He had children and infants to bless and enjoy. Christ did not father any children of His own, so having a chance to pick them up and give them a hug and bless them was a way to show His care and love for them. As He picked up each child or placed His hands on them to bless them, I wonder if He saw into the future of what they would become and how God would use them in His kingdom. As in every situation, Christ was able to use this incident as a teachable moment for us and His disciples to explore more aspects of the kingdom of God. Let's take a moment to look at Christ's teaching about His kingdom as it pertains to children.

Some observations about children

1. **Children are simple beings;** for the most part their lives are not complicated, stress filled, corporate driven, or laden with debt or obligations. What they say is normally what they mean, and their emotions are easily displayed and understandable. They do not generally have hidden agendas, ulterior motives, or devious plans in their interactions with others. With children, what you see is usually what you get.

2. **A CHILD'S ENTIRE WORLD IS ONE BASED ON UNCONDITIONAL LOVE, SECURITY, AND TRUST;** basic concepts common to people in every country and culture. As long as they have food, clothing, a safe place to sleep, and are loved, they're usually content. It's when love is withheld or safety is compromised or the basic necessities are inadequate that emotional and physical problems begin to develop. Abuse, neglect, abandonment, and fear leave emotional scars that imprint children for the rest of their lives. To see the joy in the eyes of a little girl when her rehabilitated father returns home after being separated from his family speaks volumes. Her world that was once shattered because of the lack of security, trust, and love, has been restored!

3. **CHILDREN CAN ACCEPT THINGS BASED ON FAITH THAT ADULTS STRUGGLE WITH.** Christ demonstrates this as the story continues with the rich young man who asked how to inherit eternal life. He struggled to follow Jesus because he was unwilling to release his dependency on money. Trusting God with the practical aspects of life can be a great challenge. Children accept very abstract concepts without question, until they grow older and more cynical. It's not so much that they're naive; they trust others will not lie to or deliberately mislead them. This is why the Easter Bunny, Santa Claus, the Tooth Fairy, and such exist for them; parents have said they are real, so they are. If you listen to a child's prayers, you realize he or she has no trouble believing and trusting that God will take care of him or her and provide for family needs.

4. **CHILDREN SEEM TO KNOW INTUITIVELY SOME THINGS ADULTS OFTEN FAIL TO GRASP OR ARE MORE SKEPTICAL ABOUT.** Children often sense danger, unsafe people, and others' emotions more readily than many adults because they are focused on people's facial expressions and body cues, rather than distractions. Children also will typically have a more positive outlook on life and the future because they've no reason to doubt everything will work out for the best.

5. **CHILDREN ARE MORE LIKELY TO SEE THINGS AS BLACK OR WHITE** or right or wrong and tend to rationalize less than adults. When children see a beggar on the sidewalk, they often spontaneously want to give some coins to help. Mom or Dad will immediately come up with several reasons why that would not be a good idea without ever having a conversation with the individual. I can't tell you how many times my children have reminded me to wear my seat belt while driving, or shamed me for trying to sneak through a yellow light at an intersection. How many times have you heard your children cry foul and say, "But that's not *fair*"? They like justice and equity when this is not always possible.

Of course, there are always exceptions to these observations, but exactly what is it that the Lord is trying to tell us about child-like faith? If Christ says it's impossible to enter the kingdom of heaven unless one comes as a child, then children have something to teach us about God and His expectations for us.

Our friend David Fresch tells us, "I think I knew God was calling me into the ministry as a child, but I didn't want to submit to that. I wanted to be an active Christian, but I did not want to work full time in ministry and not get to be in the business world. Anyway, I later went to my youth pastor after a youth group meeting and he prayed with me, along with some of the older youth, and I decided that God was calling me into the ministry. I went home and told my mother and she told me that God had told her that I was going to be called into the ministry when she was still pregnant with me, but she had never told me because she did not want to influence me. This was a nice confirmation. She actually said she did not want me to be in the ministry when she was pregnant or even when I told her because she knew that ministers can have a very hard life, but she did want me to follow God."

What the Lord Requires of Us

1. *Simply trust.*
Believing in God should not be complicated, confusing, or burdensome. As a child simply believes God hears when we pray,

protects when we ask, and provides when we have need, we also need to trust God. Oh, to be like a child in simple trust again without all the hang-ups, questioning, and what ifs! God is looking for His people to simply trust Him—with their children, finances, job, marriage, and future. "But without faith it is impossible to please Him, for he who comes to God must believe that He is, and that He is a rewarder of those who diligently seek Him" (Hebrews 11:6 NKJV).

2. *Do everything out of love.*

If we act out of obligation, jealousy, duty, guilt, or any other motivation than love, we are not representing Christ well. He expects us to love others in the same way He loves us. That's not easy to do! The unconditional love God demonstrates to us is sacrificial, unselfish, and without ulterior motives. It's something God helps us to learn as His Spirit works in us. Children don't automatically act out of love because human nature is naturally selfish and self-centered. But children know about love from their very first breath as they look into the eyes of their mother or father and feel gentle arms wrapped around them. Love motivates, sustains, enables, and nourishes us, and as we *live in love* (1 John 4:16; 2 John 1:6; Jude 1:1) we demonstrate God lives in us. "This is My commandment, that you love one another as I have loved you" (John 15:12 NKJV).

3. *Be content.*

Having traveled in many countries, I've seen children in every economic condition. It's an indictment on society when children with electronic gadgets and dozens of playthings are bored and dissatisfied while impoverished children laugh and play with a toy made from an abandoned milk jug! Contentment is an attitude from which we approach life and circumstances. Always looking for more tells God we're dissatisfied with how He has provided for us, and is often an indication that our priorities are out of sync. God promises to take care of our needs, not our *wants*. One of the greatest indictments against God's people in the

Old Testament was when their hearts turned away from God and jealously toward the nations around them. It didn't matter that God had provided for their every need: food, protection, guidance, and love. They wanted a king to lead them, to prostitute themselves to idols, and armies to protect them—like other nations. The more they rejected God, the deeper in trouble they got, and the farther away from His guiding hand they went. "Keep your lives free from the love of money and be content with what you have, because God has said, 'Never will I leave you; never will I forsake you'" (Hebrews 13:5 NIV).

4. *Live by faith.*

A person does not *have* faith—he or she *demonstrates* faith. It's not an intellectual exercise. Where do we demonstrate faith the most, if we look at the various parts of our family life? What areas require complete dependence on God—where you know the outcome is never guaranteed, but you trust God to work things out in His way, according to His will? James talks about two kinds of faith (James 2:14–26). One is a belief in God; the other is a life lived based on that belief in God. Faith is not private; it is to be acted out before a watching world.

We can determine the level of our faith by looking at our prayers. What in your prayers calls on God to intervene in your life? What do you pray that shows your children you expect God to handle things that are out of your hands? When we are in trouble, we ask God to intervene. When we are in need, we ask God to provide. When we are at a loss to know what to do, we ask God to guide. When we face an unexpected crisis, we ask God to sustain us and give us wisdom. Where we turn in times of need demonstrates whether we have faith or not. If you tell your children you will pick them up after school, they stand outside the school waiting for you because they *know* you will come. Their actions demonstrate their belief in you based on your past relationship. When we do not tithe because we think we'll be short the next month, don't pray about our circumstances, or try to hurry up situations for our benefit rather than letting God take care of things, our actions show our watching children what we believe about God. In God's kingdom, He requires His people to live by faith in Him. If God says it, we should believe it, and we should act upon it in daily life. Simple. "The righteous by faith shall live" (Hebrews 10:38 YLT).

5. *Trust the Holy Spirit.*
Christians are led by the Holy Spirit who guides, directs, and helps us daily. Christ described the Spirit as a counselor, advocate, helper, and guide. Essentially the Spirit acts in Christ's place for the believer. Do you need wisdom? The Spirit of wisdom is with you (Ephesians 1:17). Do you need strength to face difficult circumstances? The Spirit of power is with you (Romans 15:13). Do you need direction or guidance? The Spirit of truth is with you (John 16:13). If we can trust the Spirit to lead and give us His wisdom, truth, and power, we can live life according to the measure of fullness God intended (Ephesians 4:13). God tells us that the Spirit gives a variety of gifts to different people, so that together we'll have all that we need (1 Corinthians 12). The same is true in the family. We can learn to appreciate and value these differences and discover how God wants to use us uniquely in His kingdom. Trusting the Holy Spirit to guide us in our decisions and circumstances is invaluable as a family and as a church. "However, when He, the Spirit of Truth, has come, He will guide you into all truth" (John 16:13 NKJV).

6. *Know right from wrong.*
Christians who know God to be intimate, personal, and involved in their lives know He does have a best choice whenever we come to a crossroads. He will reveal His ways and His plans if we seek Him. Some people feel that because they have God's Spirit in them that whatever choice they make is OK with Him. Yet this leaves God out of the decision making. If we're completely free to choose our own course in life, there's no need for prayer or for God. God *does* have a plan for our lives. God *does* want to be intimately involved in our activities day to day. We are perfectly

able to choose what toothpaste we want, or what car to drive, or what to make for dinner. In God's kingdom, however, discovering what He wants is always best. "Seek the LORD and His strength; seek His face evermore!" (1 Chronicles 16:11 NKJV). He alone can change hearts, function outside of our limitations, and know the future and the plans He has for us (Jeremiah 29:11). Psalm 37:23 (GNT) states: "The LORD guides us in the way we should go and protects those who please him."

These six components demonstrate we are residents of God's kingdom. Richard Blackaby comments, "I feel like a lot of parents never teach their kids how to think. I am constantly asking my kids what they think about things and pushing them to think more deeply. I try to talk with them about what is happening around them. When a friend at church makes a bad decision, we'll talk about it and try to think through with the kids what went wrong. We don't do this to be critical but to learn from others' mistakes and successes. As a result, our kids have developed some pretty strong convictions, which I believe has protected them from a lot of hurts." □

VALUING CHILDREN

And He sat down, called the twelve, and said to them, "If anyone desires to be first, he shall be last of all and servant of all." Then He took a little child and set him in the midst of them. And when He had taken him in His arms, He said to them, "Whoever receives one of these little children in My name receives Me; and whoever receives Me, receives not Me but Him who sent Me" (Mark 9:35–37 NKJV; see also Matthew 18:2–5).

esus had traveled to Capernaum to where Peter's house was located. Here Peter's family lived along with his mother-in-law (Matthew 8:14) whom Jesus had healed of a fever. The Bible indicates He took a small child into His lap and embraced it. I want to believe it was Peter's child, though the Bible is not clear. At least we know children were completely comfortable around Christ and He was affectionate to them. Let's say it was one of Peter's children (also a nephew or niece of Andrew). Can you imagine honoring a child like that in front of all these hardworking men? They might have laughed as Christ picked up the child and embraced it. But then came the rebuke. You see, as they had been walking on the road to Peter's house, they had been arguing about who would be the greatest in Christ's kingdom. When Christ asked them what it was they had been discussing so heatedly, they hung their heads in shame without reply (Mark 9:34). The enacted parable, part rebuke and part teaching, would have made quite an impression on them. No doubt every time they looked at this same child they were reminded again of Christ's lesson on humility and service to all. But there was a second lesson to learn: how His disciples were to regard others, particularly those young in the faith.

We Are to Be God's Ambassadors to Children

Christ speaks in terms of a legal representative or an ambassador when He says, "Whoever receives one of these little children in My name receives Me." Christ wants us to value children as He values them, and to do so brings Him great joy. As we treat children with love, care, respect, and dignity, we're doing so in the name and in the place of Christ Himself. Christ wants us to love deeply every child God puts into our family, every child who walks through our door, every teenager who flops on our couch or grazes on food from our refrigerator or pantry exactly as Christ loves them. Why? Because "such is the kingdom of God."

Every child is to be molded, shaped, and influenced by love. Would we publicly embarrass Jesus in front of His friends? I don't think so. Would we belittle Him, mock Him, or threaten Him like some do with their own children? I hope not. Would we neglect Him, reduce Him to tears for the littlest infraction, beat Him, slap Him, or manipulate Him? Heaven forbid. But that is how many children are treated today. Instead we would love Him, care for Him, praise Him, and respect and honor Him, so should we also do for those He sends to us. This, of course, does not discount our responsibility as parents to disciple, rebuke, exhort, teach, and guide our children. In this particular context, Christ would not require any of these things, though our children certainly do. But wait, there's more!

> THE CHILDREN HELPED LEAD THE MUSIC, CRAFTS, AND DRAMA. I OVERHEARD THEN FIVE-YEAR-OLD LINDSAY TELLING A NATIVE AMERICAN BOY THAT ALL HE NEEDED IN LIFE TO BE HAPPY WAS JESUS.

Mark adds, "But whoever causes one of these little ones who believe in Me to stumble, it would be better for him if a large millstone were hung around his neck, and he were thrown into the sea" (Mark 9:42 NKJV). This is strong language, but the point is clear. Leading others into sin, particularly young believers, to the point where their faith is shipwrecked or shattered is a heinous crime in the eyes of the Lord. Christ intimates that it would be better for a person to be destroyed before he or she was given a chance to destroy the faith of others. Faith is a precious thing. To deliberately or indirectly cause another believer to sin or to turn from faith in Christ brings eternal consequences. The thought here is that one should choose to face dire physical consequences before his or her actions result in irreparable spiritual consequences in others.

This passage is not necessarily speaking of children specifically, but Christ is choosing to use children to teach spiritual truths about God's kingdom. Christ often chose everyday matters to teach deeper truths to those around Him. And to use a child to teach adults spiritual truths was creative, and it elevated children to a whole new level in the minds of His followers.

Kim Gross provides a contemporary illustration with her family's mission service: "I heard that a Sunday School class was taking a family missions trip where even the children would participate. I thought if there was work the children could do, surely there was something I could do. Growing up, I had thought of missionaries as superhumans who went to live in huts in Africa to preach to natives. As I became older, I began to see people from our church commit not only to full-time service, but to short-term missions trips. I saw doctors, lawyers, and teachers spend a week or two on the missions field and then return to their regular jobs. I began to see missions work as something everyone could do."

Their young daughter Lindsay Gross comments, "Going on missions trips means a lot to me. It helps us learn the meaning of life, which is spreading the Word of God, and that some people aren't as fortunate as us."

When younger daughter Anna was a four-year-old, the Grosses decided to take a missions trip to Canada. Kim says, "We went to a First Nation reservation and did a kids club for the native children. I led the music; and although I was very nervous, it was a wonderful time. The men did construction and the children helped lead the music, crafts, and drama. Anna loved it. The next summer her question was not *if* we would go on another missions trip, but *where* would we go. This time: Arizona, where the heat reached 116 degrees during the day. The Native American children were fascinated with Anna and it helped us break the ice with them. I overheard then five-year-old Lindsay telling a Native American boy that all he needed in life to be happy was Jesus.

"Year three, I had two little girls asking where the missions trip would be, so we set off with them and our six-month-old son for South Dakota. I served in the kitchen and tried to keep one eye on the baby. My husband threatened that if we kept adding a child each year we went on a trip, he would not let me come anymore. That year we were blessed by having our oldest daughter Lindsay accept Christ. It was her third missions trip.

"Tennessee and Oklahoma were our fourth and fifth trips, but we haven't added any more children. When my three-year-old son and four-year-old daughter play pretend at home, they pack a suitcase, get in their plastic Dora the Explorer car, and go on a missions trip. The long-term impact on our family is that we've learned to be God's servants. When I think of the trip to Canada, I think of Lindsay scrubbing the floor of a church basement with a smile on her face. The kids really enjoy being servants on these trips (even if they forget how when it comes time for chores at home). It has also helped to remind us that telling others about Jesus is not reserved for the superhuman career missionary in Africa. God has called us each to tell others about Jesus, whether on the missions field or at home."

Gary Gross says, "Our family missions trips have allowed us to remain focused on what is important in life—God's love, family, and serving others. In our day-to-day lives, it is easy to lose focus on those three things and get caught up in work, school events, social activities, finances, etc. Giving a week each summer has given us an anchor point—a time in the near past and the near future where all that matters is God's love, family, and serving others." □

GOD'S PLANS FOR CHILDREN

*C*hildren have played a significant role in God's plans throughout history. Whenever God had in mind to do something in history to impact mankind, a child was born that God intended to use in a mighty way years later.

■ God had every intention of freeing His people from Egyptian slavery, so a baby was born 80 years earlier and placed in a small ark in the Nile River by his parents, in order to save his life.

- God wanted to demonstrate His vast love for the world, so He determined to create a nation through which He could reveal Himself to the world. A child, Isaac, was born to an elderly couple who would in turn have a child named Jacob who would grow to father 12 sons, from whom the Israel's 12 tribes descended. A lineage was formed through these people leading to a family to whom His own Son would be given (Genesis 29–30).
- Before John the Baptist could come saying, "Repent, for the kingdom of heaven is at hand" (Matthew 3:2 NKJV), he had to be born into a family. God intended to call him into service for the King of kings and the Lord of lords to prepare the hearts of His people for the Messiah.
- Before Gideon could be called into God's service to lead the Israelites against the Midianite forces, he first had to be born and raised with his family in a home (Judges 6).

It is sometimes difficult to look at your toddler or teenager and see a great leader or influential person God wants to use mightily in His kingdom. But a home just like yours is where such leaders and people of influence come from. Some of those traits that greatly annoy you and test your patience today may be the very traits that will cause them to stand firm and navigate various trials later in life. Helping your children come to the knowledge of God early in their lives will give them a great advantage later on in life. It is God's grace that sees the potential of what each child can become.

- We see a baby. God sees a king.
- We see a toddler. God sees a missionary.
- We see a teenager. God sees a Christian CEO of an international corporation with worldwide influence.

We have no idea what God has in mind to do with our children. We simply must raise them, anticipating that God will call them in some way to serve Him. Our primary responsibility is to prepare them so they will be ready when God calls them according to His plans for their lives.

Moses (Exodus 2):
When God Spares a Child, It's for a Reason

Moses is introduced to us as a three-month-old baby. His mother, Jochebed, defied the king's decrees and rather than handing her son over to be killed, hid him from the authorities. In doing so, she put the lives of her entire family in jeopardy to save the life of her baby. She had no idea her God-inspired act of defiance and courage would save the life of arguably the greatest leader God's people would ever know. Moses's older sister, Miriam, protected him as an infant and served with him as an adult (Exodus 15:20). His older brother, Aaron, would become the first High Priest before God on behalf of the nation of Israel. The Scriptures are silent on Moses's parents after his relocation to the Egyptian palace. The hardship which slaves endured meant they generally didn't live long. We don't know if they were alive to see their dream of their children's freedom from slavery realized. Nevertheless, they had a tremendous impact on their early lives. Moses was well aware he was a Hebrew and that he served a different God than his adoptive mother's Egyptian family. When God was ready to reveal Himself to His people, Moses was the only descendant of Israel who could have voluntarily left Egypt to find God in the wilderness. All the others were confined with chains and taskmasters. A baby placed in an ark of reeds and tar would one day see the ark of the covenant crafted of gold and acacia wood by the hands of free Jews. His own two sons, Gershon and Eliezer, would also follow after their father and continue in the priestly tribe of Levi in service to the Lord (1 Chronicles 23:14–15).

My mother tells the story of her brush with death when she was five years old. She was rushed to the hospital with a ruptured appendix; and although the doctors fought to save her life, no one thought she would survive. Her mother (Carrie Wells) never left her side and continued to pray over her even when she slipped into a coma. When my mother finally awakened and began to improve, she remembers my grandmother's words, "Marilynn, God has saved your life for a purpose. You must always do whatever He wants you to do." Mom says that day she committed the rest of her life to God's service and to follow Him wherever He led.

Joseph (Genesis 37): Never Discount Children's Dreams

We first encounter Joseph at 17 years of age as he tended flocks with his brothers. God began to work in his life, giving him dreams of what was to come, though he was not yet able to understand. He found little support from his family who mocked and ridiculed him ("Here comes the dreamer!" in Genesis 37:19) and, for the most part, despised this impertinent lad. But God had plans for him. Joseph grew up in what could easily be called a dysfunctional home. His father, Jacob, had multiple wives who vied for his attention and whose sons were desperately jealous of Joseph and Benjamin, the sons of Jacob's favorite wife, Rachel (Genesis 37:4). The fact that she had died in childbirth made these two boys even more special. Jacob unwisely used Joseph to spy on his brothers and showered gifts on him while the others seemed all but neglected by their father. Had Joseph's family actually listened to what the boy was saying and not been jealous or insulted by his dreams, they could have been willing participants in the wonderful plans of God. Instead, they were unwitting players in a drama that God alone crafted. As Joseph later said to his brothers who sold him into slavery, "But as for you, you meant evil against me; but God meant it for good, in order to bring it about as it is this day, to save many people" (Genesis 50:20 NKJV). The lad whom everyone dismissed became the wisest man in the land and second in command over all of Egypt (Genesis 41:40). The forgotten younger brother survived to hold the lives of his own brothers in his hand. How many parents discount the dreams, insights, and heart desires of their children instead of inquiring of the Lord as to what it all may mean? How many brothers and sisters would treat their siblings differently if they knew what the Lord had in mind to do with them?

Samson (Judges 13–16):
God Prepares Children for His Purposes

Little is known of Samson's childhood, but we do know that his parents were specially chosen by God and given a very specific promise about their son ("He shall begin to deliver Israel out of the hand of the Philistines" in Judges 13:5 NKJV) and very specific instructions by an angel of God on how to raise him according to the Nazirite laws. We also know according to Judges 13:24–25 (NKJV) that as Samson "grew, and the Lord blessed him. And the Spirit of the Lord began to move upon him." We can't say exactly what this looked like or what was going on in this young man, but we know at least that God was present in his life. Many feel this was the time Samson developed his passion to free his people from the oppression of the Philistines. He distinguished himself as a young man full of passion and single-minded purpose. As with most of the people recorded in the Bible, his parents recede into the background and are not heard of again. As the story of Samson unfolds, several serious character cracks appear. But God used these flaws to bring about His purposes (Judges 14:4). He was misunderstood by his own countrymen and betrayed by them (Judges 15:11–13). Yet even this misunderstood servant of God was used as a judge over Israel and defender against the Philistines to accomplish God's purposes (Judges 15:20). It's incredible for parents to know God has chosen a child for His special purposes. Though this is a great honor, it's no easy responsibility. Raising a child in the fear and understanding of the Lord while knowing he will likely have a difficult road ahead of him can be difficult for any parent. It's painful to see your child face fierce opposition to what he or she understands God calling him or her to do. Samson's entire life and ministry was to annoy and defeat the enemies oppressing God's people. His life was in constant danger. His future was dubious at best. His parents had to trust that the God who called him into service would sustain and protect him. There were other servants of God in the Bible who also had self-destructive characters, such as King Saul, King David, and Jonah, yet God used them significantly. We don't know what Samson could have accomplished had he honored the Lord in every area of his life and remained faithful to his calling, but his reputation as a mighty man of God persists.

Samuel (1 Samuel 1): Trusting God with Our Children

Samuel's mother, Hannah, vowed that if God would give her a child, she would give him back to serve in God's temple (1 Samuel 1–2). God honored her request, and she was faithful to bring the boy to the prophet Eli after he was old enough to enter the Lord's service (1 Samuel 2:11). It must have been a difficult decision for her and many probably counseled her against her sacrifice, but God honored her devotion and chose this son to have a tremendous role before His people and a continuing impact on the generations.

Each year, Hannah faithfully brought to the temple a new set of clothes for her son, Samuel, and visited with him. As time went by, she was able to bring his three younger brothers and two sisters (1 Samuel 2:21) with her to meet their oldest brother. The Bible tells us that Samuel, even as a young child, ministered before the Lord (1 Samuel 2:18) and continued to grow and serve in the temple. In fact, the Scriptures say Samuel "grew in stature, and in favor both with the Lord and men" (1 Samuel 2:26 NKJV). God spoke with Samuel as a boy (1 Samuel 3) and gave him important prophecies and understandings for the people to hear. "And all Israel from Dan to Beersheba knew that Samuel had been established as a prophet of the Lord" (1 Samuel 3:20 NKJV). It was rare in those days to hear a word from the Lord, and it was even rarer to hear prophetic messages coming from someone so young. But God had decided, "I will raise up for Myself a faithful priest who shall do according to what is in My heart and in My mind" (1 Samuel 2:35 NKJV).

Giving our children to the Lord is no easy thing. Trusting them and their future completely into His hands may cause fear and anxiety. However, letting them go into God's hands is so much more secure than keeping them under our watchful eye. We can only imagine how proud Hannah would have been to know that God was using her son as His prophet to guide and protect His people.

David (1 Samuel 16ff.): God Shapes His Servants from a Young Age

David, the youngest of eight sons of Jesse, began as a shepherd boy tending his father's sheep near Bethlehem (1 Samuel 16:11). He guided them to graze in green pastures, beside still waters, and protected them from predators. We learn that even at a young age he had the strength and fortitude to single-handedly defeat both a bear and a lion with only his shepherd's staff and a sling (1 Samuel 17:34–35). This teenager displayed not only great courage beyond his years in defeating the seasoned warrior and giant Goliath (1 Samuel 17), he also demonstrated an uncanny dependency on God for protection and strength. His relationship with God would carry him through many battles as a soldier and later provide the wisdom he would need to lead the Israelites as their king. The greatest description of David comes from the prophet Samuel who declared to King Saul, "But now your kingdom shall not continue. The LORD has sought for Himself a man after His own heart, and the LORD has commanded him to be commander over His people, because you have not kept what the LORD commanded you" (1 Samuel 13:14 NKJV). To be known as a man after God's heart was a tremendous affirmation of David's dedication and devotion to God. No other person in the Bible is given this description.

Throughout David's life, he would face many more challenges, including attempted assassination, concerted efforts to overthrow his rule, adultery, murder, and great disappointment in not being able to build a temple for God's dwelling place. Nevertheless, David maintained the same devotion to God in maturity as he had in his youth. The young boy who tended the sheep for his earthly father was given the responsibility to watch over the entire nation of Israel for his heavenly Father. His life was not trouble free; it was, however, purposeful and rich. Not many people in the Bible were at the same time a musician, a venerable warrior, a king, and a servant of God like David.

Daniel and Friends (Daniel 1ff.): Strong Convictions Come from Strong Foundations

Daniel (Belteshazzar) and his three friends, Hananiah (Shadrach), Mishael (Meshach), and Azariah (Abed-Nego) were taken into captivity from their homeland and deported to Babylon under the rule and command of Nebuchadnezzar, king of Babylon. They were mere teenagers when they were brought to serve in the king's court. The Bible tells us they were bright, healthy, good-looking, knowledgeable, and quick learners (Daniel 1:4). But these four friends were also faithful to the Lord. One would think that once teenagers get away from home, they throw off parental constraints and enjoy whatever temptations and enticements are available. But their parents had instilled in them a powerful sense of how to honor God and they did not depart from this. They distinguished themselves as having uncommon good sense, good morals, and integrity—characteristics apparently lacking in their fellow captives taken with them to Babylon. When the king finally had an opportunity to personally examine his court conscripts, he found those who had been faithful to God were head and shoulders above their peers but also above all the existing intelligentsia of his realm. "And in all matters of wisdom and understanding about which the king examined them, he found them ten times better than all the magicians and astrologers who were in all his realm" (Daniel 1:20 NKJV). Every parent hopes that their teenagers remember their upbringing and honor their family values when they are away from home. These four friends were a great support to one another and remained faithful even when faced with tremendous adversity (i.e., fiery furnace, Daniel 3:17–30ff.; and lions' den, Daniel 6:10–28ff.).

I (Tom) had a fairly sheltered childhood and had not been around any of the usual vices and temptations common to teenagers. Even in high school I only participated in church-sponsored activities. Then came college. I auditioned for the university wind ensemble and was chosen as sixth player in the trumpet section (there were only six of us!). On our first road trip as a band, we went to a number of small towns to perform concerts and lead band clinics. We traveled on a big tour bus and stayed in hotels.

My first night in one of the hotels, I was rooming with three other band members, but I had no idea what I was about to face. My roommates purchased alcohol as soon as the bus unloaded. Then I was locked out of my room for two hours while another roommate was using drugs in the bathroom. Later that night after I had gone to bed, the door opened, and along with two of my inebriated roommates came four tipsy girls who "wanted to get to know me better." Drugs, alcohol, and womanizing all in the first night! Many of the band members cast off all restraints, so I had to choose quickly where I stood and who I wanted to be as a young adult. I declined the offer to "get to know" the girls better and the next day requested a room change for the remainder of the tour.

The values my family instilled and my commitment to personal purity trumped the powerful temptations and God placed me with a strong Christian friend to support me for the rest of the tour.

Paul's Nephew (Acts 23:12–22): Children Can Play Significant Roles

Paul's sister's family lived in Jerusalem where Paul also had studied as a young man. Throughout Paul's missionary travels, he had accumulated a lot of enemies who tracked him like assassins trying to take his life (Acts 14:19). By Acts 21, his enemies discovered him in the Temple in Jerusalem and caused quite a ruckus, so much so that Paul was dragged outside the Temple and nearly beaten to death by a mob. He was arrested by the commander of the Roman troops, to save his life, and led to safety. But the mob persisted and the religious leaders were so incensed by his presence, they plotted to kill him during transport the next day. Paul's nephew was in the right place at the right time to overhear the 40 men vow to kill Paul or die trying. Paul's nephew informed Paul, who sent him to the commander, who arranged for safe transport out of Jerusalem to Caesarea that very night. We have no more information about Paul's nephew. We don't even know his name. We do know he saved his Uncle Paul's life that night. God chose to use a young boy in saving one of God's most effective missionaries and author of at least 13 of our New Testament books.

Christ (Luke 1; Matthew 1): The Hope of the World in a Child

"For unto us a Child is born, unto us a Son is given; and the government will be upon His shoulder; and His name will be called Wonderful, Counselor, Mighty God, Everlasting Father, Prince of Peace" (Isaiah 9:6 NKJV). Isaiah prophesied that a child would be born that would be like none born before Him or after. This child would be both God and man and would establish a kingdom like the world had never seen. Hundreds of years later in the City of David, in Bethlehem of Judea, a child was born of Mary and placed in a manger filled with straw. This child would change both heaven and earth for all time. While the angels rejoiced, the demons shuddered. Even as He grew, his parents saw that He was very different from other children. Once when they were more than a day's journey toward home after celebrating Passover in Jerusalem, they realized their 12-year-old was not with them. They searched among their relatives for their firstborn son only to find He was not with anyone in their traveling party. When they arrived back in the congested city of Jerusalem, they finally located Him sitting among the teachers, debating with them in the Temple. The Bible says, "And all who heard Him were astonished at His understanding and answers" (Luke 2:47 NKJV). His only reply to His parents when they expressed their frustration with Him was, "Why did you seek me? Did you not know that I must be about My Father's business?" (Luke 2:49 NKJV). Then the Scriptures say, "And Jesus increased in wisdom and stature, and in favor with God and men" (Luke 2:52 NKJV), much in the same way Samuel was described as a young man (1 Samuel 2:26). To have a child grow in their standing both before God and those in the community is a true blessing. It means that child's relationship with God is showing through his or her actions and in relation to others. □

GOD AT WORK IN YOUR FAMILY

Now remember what you were, my friends, when God called you. From the human point of view few of you were wise or powerful or of high social standing. God purposely chose what the world considers nonsense in order to shame the wise, and He chose what the world considers weak in order to shame the powerful. He chose what the world looks down on and despises and thinks is nothing, in order to destroy what the world thinks is important. This means that no one can boast in God's presence (1 Corinthians 1:26–29 GNT).

*I*t may be a stretch for some parents to look at their children and imagine that God would use them significantly in His kingdom work. The messy room, disrespectful remarks, bad attitude, and the shyness or even social ineptness seem insurmountable obstacles. Children always grow up and can amaze you with their change in behavior, attitude, and social graces. Never underestimate God for He has often chosen the insignificant and lowly to accomplish His greatest works. Seeing our children as God sees them may be at times one of the greatest challenges parents face.

Sharon and Robbie Moore write: "As we look back, we see where missions trips have influenced our daughters. For instance, Becca went on her first missions trip when she was five. With her twin sisters, Beth and Baileigh, then three, traveled like champs to Canada for their first missions trip. Along the way, all three made friends with a woman whose husband was severely injured in an accident. They prayed for her husband and also the woman. They were not told to, they just did.

Becca, now nine, attended the team meeting for the 2008 trip and had great hopes of going to Boston, an area rich is history, her favorite subject in school. Upon discussion, the possibility of a trip to Tulsa, Oklahoma, arose. After hearing Mimi Holland's description of the needs for both areas, Becca stood and said, 'Mimi, I really want to go to Boston, but Tulsa needs us more. I vote we go to Tulsa.' Wow, what a proud mom I was sitting there. What better way to teach your children how to minister and love others?

"Interestingly, children open doors to homes and families that would normally not be receptive to hearing from strangers. Children know no prejudices; they don't rule people out because of appearance, culture, or creed. They just see other children. When children attend our Kids Club meetings, their parents come to see what is happening. This opens the door to share the gospel with them. It gives parents an opportunity to share their God stories and Christ with others.

"Family missions gives families time together in a very hectic world. It's a time out of the hustle and bustle of everyday life that people simply consider a given. It shows how God's love is for everyone—the weak, the strong, the sick, the elderly, and the lost." ☐

FAMILY-TIME REFLECTIONS

1. Don't discount what God may be telling your child. Might he or she become a missionary? Doctor? Pastor?

2. Expect that God has called each of your children into His service in one form or another and prepare them now for what they may face in the days to come.

3. Giving our children to the Lord is no easy thing.

4. Be ready for your children to face opposition and to be misunderstood by others.

5. Know that when your children are serving the Lord as He has called them to do that they are in the center of His will and could never be happier.

■ ■ ■

"All the ends of the earth will remem-

ber and turn to the LORD, and all the

families of the nations will bow down

before him, for dominion belongs

to the LORD and he rules over the

nations"

(Psalm 22:27–28 NIV).

■ ■ ■

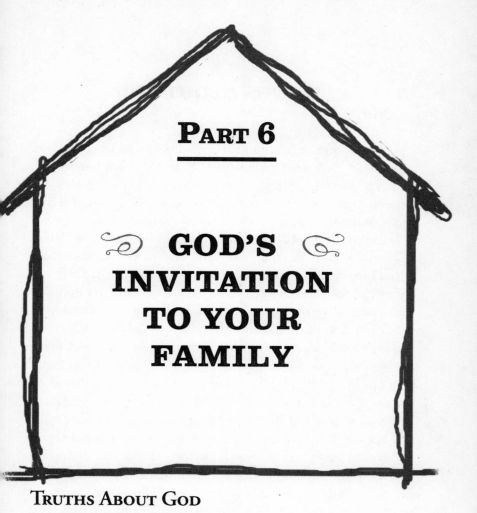

PART 6

GOD'S INVITATION TO YOUR FAMILY

TRUTHS ABOUT GOD

A phone call from Kim jarred me awake late one night. "We need you to pray!" Kim said. I was out of town and our 14-year-old son, Matt, was communicating over the Internet with a friend. The friend confided that he was angry at life, wishing his life was over, and then suddenly broke off communication. The week before he had taken a bottle of pills and his stomach had to be pumped, so Matt told Kim, who contacted the friend's mother and emergency services were dispatched. He was so violent the police needed to restrain him before transporting him to the hospital. At 1:30 A.M., Kim called me as she and Matt headed to meet the friend at the hospital. By all accounts, our son was incredibly helpful in calming his friend down and convincing him to remain under hospital care. God had brought this friend into our lives eight months earlier when he and Matt played on the same basketball team for which I volunteered as assistant coach. God had laid this friend on Kim's heart and our family had been praying for him for some time as he had a troubled past and was currently in foster care. We knew God led us to develop a relationship with him for a reason, but we had no idea how pivotal this relationship would be. God rarely gives us the big picture until we have been faithful in the small things first. But when we see what God had intended to happen down the road, we are so grateful He let us be a part of His plans. ☐

GOD HAS BEEN WORKING
IN YOUR FAMILY ALREADY

*T*here are certain things we know about God, things that are always true no matter what.

1. GOD LOVES PEOPLE. God's nature is love and everything He does comes from the basis of pure love (Exodus 34:6; 1 John 4:16). If we ever question God's love or motivation for what He does, we only have to look at the Cross and know the question of His love for us was settled through the sacrifice of His Son, Jesus Christ.

2. GOD WANTS TO REDEEM THE LOST. God is still in the business of saving lost and broken people of all ages and bringing them into His kingdom (2 Peter 3:9). Since the beginning of humankind, God has continuously sought to restore the relationship with us that was broken by our sin. He has never stopped pursuing those who are lost.

3. GOD USES HIS PEOPLE. We are His best strategy to accomplish His will (2 Corinthians 5:18–20). All the stories in the Bible are about people through whom God worked. This is His pattern in the Bible and it continues today.

4. GOD IS ALWAYS AT WORK. The Spirit of God is active in varying degrees in the hearts of people around us (Philippians 2:13; John 5:17). Like plants, some people are ripe and ready to enter the kingdom, others still need much watering and care, and still others with hard hearts need the gentle rains to begin softening the soil so they can receive the seeds the Spirit wants to plant in their hearts.

5. GOD IS PREPARING HIS PEOPLE. There are specific activities He has planned in advance for His people to do (Ephesians 2:10). He is the master planner, the architect of eternity, and it's ours to discover what it is God has in mind for us to do with Him.

Knowing these five things should help us keep proper perspective in our lives and in our activities. They can guide our thinking, planning, schedules, and our focus as we go about our daily lives. ☐

GOD IS IN CONTROL

*T*he longer we walk with God, the more we come to understand that He truly is in control of our lives and circumstances.

Not only is your family important to God, but it is His desire to use your family to influence others for His kingdom work right where you are and in places you have yet to go. We may think we have control over our lives, and we may think it is our plans that are working out, but the Bible says differently. Look at Proverbs 16:9 in several translations:

- "You may make your plans, but God directs your actions." (GNT)
- "A man's heart plans his way, but the LORD directs his steps." (NKJV)
- "In his heart a man plans his course, but the LORD determines his steps." (NIV)
- "A man's mind plans his way, but the LORD directs his steps and makes them sure." (AMP)

Every aspect of our lives and history, men and women and children, has God's fingerprint. "The LORD guides us in the way we should go and protects those who please him" (Psalm 37:23 GNT). Whether you know it or not, God has been guiding you to where you are right now. Yes, each one of us has choices. We can choose to sin and rebel against God and reap the consequences that brings. Neither are we robots programmed by God to fulfill His whims. But as Christians, His Spirit lives within us and He helps us to *want* to do what pleases God. He helps us to discern God's will. He helps us to make choices that are in keeping with what God has planned for us. He does this out of His great love for us and out of a deep desire for us to experience Him fully in our lives.

The home you have, the school your children attend, the neighborhood you live in, your job, the person you married, each member of your family, the church you attend, and the activities you are involved in—all have been orchestrated by God if you have trusted in Him with all your heart, sought His wisdom as you have made decisions, and acknowledged Him in all you do. The Bible tells us He will then direct your paths (Proverbs 16:3). Can you see how God has directed you down the path of your life and where it has led you? God is able to use even our biggest mistakes to bring glory to Himself.

> THE BOOK *Experiencing God* CAME NOT ONLY FROM HENRY, BUT IS THE RESULT OF YEARS OF FAITHFUL SERVICE THROUGHOUT MANY GENERATIONS. NOW HIS FIVE CHILDREN SERVE THE LORD AND SEVERAL OF HIS GRAND-CHILDREN ARE NOW SENSING GOD'S CALL.

Some people think God first began to work in the Apostle Paul's life after his encounter with Christ on the road to Damascus (Acts 22:6). This is not true. God was there at Saul's birth and as Saul grew up and went to school. God knew about Paul's academic life and his religious zeal and had a plan to redirect it, use it, and turn it into a blessing for others. The determination and stubbornness in Paul that probably drove his parents crazy as a youth was what God would use to keep him standing firm in the midst of terrible persecution and physical abuse later in life. Even the fact that Paul was a Roman citizen was going to be used by God to take the gospel message to the heart of the Roman Empire (Acts 23:11). What Paul would count as worthless (Philippians 3) God was going to use to bring Himself glory. It is a mistake to think that all of your life before becoming a Christian was wasted.

God did not at random pluck Moses off the mountainside and enlist him into His service. God had been watching Moses's life since birth and planned to use his training, background, knowledge of the desert, family heritage, and passion to help his own people in redeeming His people from a life of slavery in Egypt. Even his family lineage and the foster family in which he grew up would play a significant role in Moses's life and ministry. Have a look at your own family background and heritage. You may find notable prayer warriors, evangelists, preachers, missionaries, and faithful followers of Christ in the family tree who have carried His banner long before you were born. The promises God made to your forefathers He now applies to you and your family.

My father, Henry Thomas Blackaby, came from a long line of committed followers of Christ. His father was a banker and a church planter. His brother William is a faithful layman in his church—two of his children serve on church staffs and one is president of a theological seminary in Canada. Lorimar and Olive Baker, my father's uncle and aunt, were missionaries to China; and Lorimar was the pastor who baptized him as a teenager. His great-uncle, Frederick E. Blackaby, went to Spurgeon's College for pastors from 1878 to 1881 and pastored several churches.

Henry's in-laws were also faithful in their devotion to God. His mother- and father-in-law served in their church for decades before going to Zambia, Africa, as missionaries for more than five years. His sister-in-law and her husband served as missionaries to Eastern Europe for many years before he became president of a theological seminary in Prague. Henry's brother-in-law and his wife have also faithfully served as pastor and professor in many churches and taught in several theological seminaries.

The book *Experiencing God* came not only from Henry, but is the result of years of faithful service throughout many generations that have influenced his life. Now his five children serve the Lord as pastors, professors, missionaries, and ministers; and several of his grandchildren are now sensing God's call on their lives in full-time Christian ministry. Many people can look back at their family relations and find some who were faithful to God. The prayers of our family and relatives can leave a legacy of influence on future generations even long after they have passed away.

God has worked through family lines in the past, and He continues to do so today. For those who do not have a family history of faithful followers of Christ, they have the privilege of beginning the heritage for their own family and those who follow after them. We can never overestimate the impact our faithfulness will have on the generations who follow in our footsteps. "Remember that the LORD your God is the only God and that he is faithful. He will keep his covenant and show his constant love to a thousand generations of those who love him and obey his commands" (Deuteronomy 7:9 GNT).

God's Perspective Is Crucial

We must be on the lookout for God-ordained circumstances, because if we miss them, we have missed a wonderful kingdom opportunity where God wants us to join Him in what He is doing in the lives of those around us. "If anyone serves Me, let him follow Me; and where I am, there My servant will be also. If anyone serves Me, him My Father will honor" (John 12:26 NKJV). Have a look at these verses below and notice the attitude of God's people in the Bible:

- "Then Mary said, 'Behold the maidservant of the Lord!'" (Luke 1:38 NKJV).
- "I commend to you Phoebe our sister, who is a servant of the church in Cenchrea" (Romans 16:1 NKJV).
- "Tychicus, a beloved brother, faithful minister, and fellow servant in the Lord" (Colossians 4:7 NKJV).

- "Epaphras, . . . a bondservant of Christ, greets you" (Colossians 4:12 NKJV).
- "Paul, a servant of God and an apostle of Jesus Christ" (Titus 1:1 NKJV).
- "James, a handservant of God and of the Lord Jesus Christ" (James 1:1 NKJV).
- "Simon Peter, a bondservant and apostle of Jesus Christ" (2 Peter 1:1 NKJV).
- "Jude, a bondservant of Jesus Christ, and brother of James" (Jude 1:1 NKJV).

Did you make the connection in these verses? God's people are His *servants*. Servants not only serve, but they seek the Master's will. In other words, the servants do not have to guess at what pleases their master; they simply have to ask him what his will is. Servants don't spend time dreaming up dreams and coming up with visions for the master to bless; instead they go to the master who reveals to them his thoughts and desires. The very nature of servants is to serve their master. They can be busy doing lots of great and wonderful things, but if they are not accomplishing what the master has given them to do, they simply have disobeyed the master, no matter how good their intentions.

God's people need not be running around trying to find good things to do for God. Instead we should be waiting upon our Master, seeking His heart to find out what His will is. We should be watching to see where God is working around us and joining Him in what He has purposed to do through us. Rather than asking God *why* a situation was allowed to happen, we need always to ask God *what* it is He has in mind to do in and through the situation to bring glory to Himself.

Ask Him what He has in mind to do *through* you to make you into a person of spiritual influence. As God's people, we understand that nothing is coincidental for the child of God. God is completely able to work in and through any circumstance at any time, anywhere, both the good and the bad. □

GOD AT WORK AROUND US

*T*he challenge for us today is not so much in accepting that God is in control of our lives; rather, it's trying to figure out what exactly He is up to! Take a few moments to stop and consider the details of where God has led you and your family. Think about how God has been involved in your life now and even before you may have even acknowledged He existed. Remember, everything God does is entirely intentional. Keep in mind that this is not simply about being busy as a Christian or about doing lots of good works. It is about enjoying the life God has prepared for you and your family. It is about experiencing the thrill of God working through you to change lives forever. In fact, it truly isn't about us at all; it is about God and what He wants to accomplish on earth before His Son returns. When you look at the following questions, reflect on what it is that God may be up to in your life and how He may want to work through your family to be a blessing to others around you. What you see below is meant to open your mind to possibilities of what God may be doing in you and wants to do through you.

1. WHERE YOU LIVE

- Are you located in a neighborhood where people can easily gather?
- Is your house big enough to host a small Bible study or a youth social event?
- Do you have any extra rooms to use for ministry purposes? (i.e., hosting traveling missionaries/evangelists, keeping troubled teens, giving temporary shelter to battered women)
- What do you think God had in mind when He led you to this particular house?

A widow offered her spare room to Elijah to stay in when he was in the vicinity of Zarephath. In return, Elijah blessed her home with a never-ending supply of oil and flour: "The bowl will not run out of flour or the jar run out of oil before the day that I, the LORD, send rain" (1 Kings 17:14 GNT). When her son grew ill and died, Elijah raised him from the dead. God knew the widow would need Elijah's intervention. It is fortuitous that she was obedient to God and welcomed His servant into her home.

2. YOUR HOME

- Have you dedicated your home to the Lord for His use and His purposes?
- Is your home a meeting place for your children's friends or a place where they feel accepted, welcome, and loved?
- When people come into your home, is it obvious to them that God is important to your family?
- Do you regularly have people in your home to encourage, pray for, or disciple them?
- Would you say the things in your home bear witness to your devotion to God?
- Is your home a museum of artifacts and precious belongings or a place where people are more important than things, where people laugh and hug, and where lasting memories are created?
- What do you think the Lord is most pleased with about your home?

Our home in Stavanger, Norway, was called the PMC (Pastoral Ministry Center) which housed our family of five, the youth pastor's family, and the church office on three levels. We hosted home groups, praise team practices, Bible studies, prayer meetings, church barbecues, and had dozens of kids over for sleepovers! We protected our family life while at the same time offering our house as a blessing to God's people. We have so many memories now of families who shared a meal with us, came for birthday parties, or visited over coffee. These were times that shaped our children's lives as they grew and built in them a love for God's people. When we moved to a smaller home in Canada, we had to downsize what we were able to do with our home. We're no longer able to invite the whole church over, but we share it with smaller groups and individuals, enjoying the opportunity to bless others.

3. KNOWING YOUR NEIGHBORS

- What are your neighbors' life situations?
- What are your neighbors' needs or concerns?
- Are your neighbors believers and do they attend a church?
- Are there common interests you have with them that would be a bridge to ministering to them, or ways you could minister with them to others in your community?
- Would their children go with your family to church or kids' programs if they don't have a church home?
- How could your family be praying for each of your neighbors right now?
- Would they be interested in meeting in your home to discuss the Bible if you suggested it, even if they attend church elsewhere?
- Do you know your paperboy or papergirl and mail carrier personally?
- Are you being salt and light in your neighborhood right now?
- What do you think God had in mind when He placed you in this neighborhood?

4. WHO YOU ARE

- What are the special interests of each family member? (music, sports, art, speaking, mime, math, crafts, etc.) How do you think God could use these things to influence others for His kingdom?
- In what areas do family members excel? Could God use these areas for His purposes?
- How are family members gifted? (encouragement, administration, teaching, prayer, wisdom, etc.)

- Is there anything or anyone that God has laid on their hearts or given them a burden for?
- Can you look at each person in your family and see how God is working in his or her life and is helping him or her to grow in the Lord?
- Who are their friends? Can you name them?
- Can you see the possibility of beginning a Bible study or kids' club with your children's friends?
- What do you think God had in mind when He placed each one of the members in your family?
- Do you sense that any of your children have been specially called by God to serve Him in a particular way?
- How are you praying for your family members right now?

5. Your workplace

- Do you understand that God has placed you in your workplace for a special reason?
- Have you asked God how He wants to use you as salt and light where you work?
- Does your job allow you or require you to travel to places where missionaries may not be allowed to go?
- Are there certain people at work that God wants to speak to through you?
- Are there other believers at work with whom you might have a Bible study or begin to join with to pray for others at work?
- Is there someone with whom you connect that your family may befriend?
- Is there someone at work with no close family to whom you may be able to become family?
- What do you think God had in mind when He brought you to this particular place of work?

6. Your circle of influence

- In what organizations, clubs, teams, etc., are you a member, participant, coach, or leader?

- Do you see that God may have placed you in these organizations/groups/teams for a specific reason?
- Do you see how your Christian influence can have an impact on others in the group?
- Are there other parents at your children's school who would be willing to pray with you for the children, school, and staff?
- Are there particular groups of people in your church for whom there is no specific ministry? (i.e., handicapped, internationals, college students, teenagers, children, mothers of preschoolers, new Christians, etc.)
- What relatives or family members do you have that still have not made a commitment to Christ? Is your family praying regularly for them?
- Are there specific parents that you always see at your children's sports events? Is God bringing them into your path for a reason?
- Do you have the time and interest to volunteer in the school classroom, library, music room, etc.?
- Are there areas that are being neglected at work that you could be involved in as a ministry?
- Would there be an interest in starting a Christian businessman's/businesswoman's Bible study and encouragement group?

7. Divine encounters where family members can have an impact on others for God's kingdom
- Wrong phone numbers dialed
- Sitting by someone on the bus/train/plane/boat
- Encounters at the grocery store/bank/department store/swimming pool, etc.
- Families met while on vacation
- People you meet while at your children's games, lessons, performances, parties, school events
- Parents of your children's playmates
- People you meet during a time of crisis or in emergency situations
- Clients/patients/customers you meet through work situations

A Christian piano tuner has the opportunity to go into hundreds of private homes each year. After he tunes the pianos, he chooses to test them by playing hymns and Christian songs and then engages the owners to talk about the Lord. A physician offers to pray with her patients about serious conditions. A home renovations contractor regularly shares his faith with customers and invites them to his church if they are not attending one. A computer repairman's reputation for fixing computers quickly and treating customers fairly gives him a platform to share his faith. A coach regularly prays with his team before games and encourages a Bible study on character and personal goals. A teacher becomes aware of needs in a particular family in her school and encourages her church to address those needs at no charge. A hairdresser regularly engages her clients in conversation and shares with them about her love for the Lord.

8. OUTSIDE-THE-BOX OPPORTUNITIES FOR INFLUENCE

- Is there a prison nearby? (Bible studies, prisoner's family care, prayer for prisoners, etc.)
- Is there a food bank, women's shelter, homeless shelter, or orphanage near you? (Give Christmas gifts to women and their children; bring home people during Thanksgiving or Christmas; provide transportation to church on Sundays; become a mentor or encourager, etc.)
- Are there any ports nearby frequented by sailors or cruise ship staff?
- Do you have any resorts, cabins, campsites, or vacation spots nearby where children or teenagers spend weeks or months at a time? (children's clubs, teenage outreach events, day camps, sports camps, etc.)
- Do you know any missionaries who could use some help, supplies, prayer, or encouragement?
- Consider speaking with your city's mayor or council members regarding how you can pray for them.

When we finally come to understand how every aspect of our lives—home, neighborhood, office, hobbies, even our vacations—can be an avenue through which God can have an impact on the lives of those around us, we will begin to see situations and circumstances through His eyes. Every person we sit by, every salesman who comes to our door, every client we meet, every parent we cheer with at a ball game may, in fact, be God's appointment for us that day.

One day Jesus met a man in Jericho sitting up in a tree. His name was Zacchaeus. Most people would have kept on walking. After all, this man was considered to be a scoundrel, a thief, and a traitor. But Jesus saw him as God's *appointment* for Him that day (Luke 19). Not only was a life transformed for eternity, but Zacchaeus's change of heart would have an impact on a whole city. Another day Jesus happened across a woman drawing water from a well in the afternoon. Most men would not have stopped to talk with her, as she was a woman of questionable character shunned by the townspeople. But to Christ, she was His *appointment* for that afternoon (John 4). Not only was her life changed that day, but a whole town was affected by her transformed heart. One day Ananias of Damascus was minding his own business when the Spirit of God directed him to Judas's house on Straight Street. There he met his *appointment*, Saul of Tarsus, who had been blinded by Christ's glory. Not only was Saul's heart changed that day, but through him, the gospel was taken to much of the known world. As Philip was walking along the road, he noticed a foreigner reading the Scriptures. He realized this was God's afternoon *appointment* for him. He climbed up onto the chariot, explained the truths of the Scripture to this government official from Ethiopia, leading him to understand the gospel, and even baptized him! Our whole life will be a series of God-ordained appointments if we have eyes to see what God is up to around us.

The Bible is full of such appointments where God wanted to influence certain people through His servants. Samuel sought out a young shepherd boy named David who was destined to become a king. Paul sought out a young believer named Timothy who was destined to become a pastor in a church Paul planted. Jesus sought out 12 men who would become His disciples and later His apostles. Paul found a businesswoman named Lydia by a river near Philippi who would become the first believer in a newly established church. Joshua's two spies came across a woman named Rahab in Jericho who became their protector and was later grafted into the people of Israel to become great-great-grand-mother to King David. As God's people, our eyes should always be open to the possibility that God is calling on us to be people of influence. What might God be up to if...

- your child brings home a friend from school;
- the high school basketball coach requests your help to nurture weaker players on your child's team;
- the parents of a bully at school call to apologize for their child's behavior toward your son or daughter;
- you are paired with two others at work to form a study group to develop proposals;
- your neighbor wants you to watch her children so she can take her husband to the emergency room at the hospital;
- you see a man sitting on the street corner with a "Will Work for Food" sign;
- you see a woman sitting in the stands, crying, where your child takes swimming lessons;
- a member of your family calls saying he or she is leaving a marriage and has nowhere to go;
- a member of your church announces he or she is responding to a call for disaster relief and needs volunteers to go and help?

Can you see how God might want to work through your family members to be of influence for Him in these situations? Mel Blackaby says, "We were encouraged to be faithful in little things like helping with a youth mission Bible study, teaching Sunday School, working with kids in Vacation Bible School, and let God increase our place of responsibility in His time and in His way. We never sought recognition or influence; we only tried to do well in whatever role God gave us. We learned to be happy with who we are and to let God affirm us rather than looking to people for affirmation." (Mel currently pastors an 8,500-member church in Jonesboro, Georgia.)

Examples of actual missions projects for families
- Softwood Framing Construction Project, Pacific Rim
- Backyard Bible Camp Projects, Ukraine
- Log Splitting Evangelism, Serbia
- Kidz Games Outreach, Australia
- Dixieland Band, Hungary
- Tokyo Santa Project, Tokyo
- Community Cleanup, Bulgaria
- Christmas in Serbia—Performing Arts
- Gujarati Muslims—Sowing Circle—Quilters, India
- English Clubs, Macedonia
- Humanitarian Aid Distribution, Macedonia
- Bible Distribution, Turkey
- Prayerwalking, Bulgaria
- GoFlyAKite, India
- Alpine Prayerwalking, Slovenia
- Fishing with Arab Men, Africa/Middle East
- Cycling for Souls!, Hungary
- Soccer Clinics for Himalayan Villagers, Nepal
- Construction, Paraguay
- *JESUS* Film Missions Trips, France/Spain

Mimi Holland of First Baptist Church, Jonesboro, Georgia, shares: "Our Young Married Sunday School Class is determined to not just *learn* the Bible but to *do* the Bible. Five years ago as we finished the study of *The Purpose-Driven Life*, we challenged our class to put into practice what we had just learned. One of the purposes we studied was service. We asked ourselves what ministry in the church no one else wanted to take on. As a class we decided to take on the nursery. Despite the fact that few of our class members had children of their own, we served faithfully as volunteers, watching other people's children so parents could worship on Sundays. Five years later, many of our class members continue to serve in the nursery. They are true servants!

"Another purpose was missions. We had been taking an offering regularly for missions, but we felt we were to do more. As young marrieds, we did not have much money, so we determined to combine vacations and missions trips wherever possible. Together we planned several missions trips as families, taking children's missions programs to native Indians in both Canada and the US, as well as helping struggling and new-start churches. We have done work projects, service projects, and kids clubs to encourage God's people, reach the lost, and serve the Lord in many places. Every child, no matter what age, has a place of service—some in drama, others in music, puppets, and games. All welcome and love on the children and adults who come. The men repair and build; the women prepare food, lead crafts, and help the children lead. It has been a joy to see a single woman bring her two nieces, grand-parents bring their grandchildren, and whole families with children as young as six months old serving together on missions.

"Often the children corner us at church asking if we have chosen our next place of ministry yet. Each year we pray about where God can use us and He always provides us with the perfect location and ministry to serve in. Our first missions trip saw 12 adults and 12 children participate. This past year we had 30 children and 25 adults go with us. It is so exciting to see what God can do when families work together. We can't wait to see how God is going to use these children who serve so faithfully for His kingdom when they become adults."

No one in God's kingdom is insignificant to God and He can choose to use anyone He wants to use to accomplish His purposes. From babies to teens to senior citizens, God has done incredible things through every age group.

Janice Davis writes: "When our oldest daughter was 5, we had a missionary come to our house for a meal. That night as we listened to her speak, Lynne wrote a note to the missionary that she thought she might want to be a missionary too. We were unable to get the note to the missionary that night. Lynne cried and cried. I kept the note. As she turned 10, she made a public decision to be a missionary. At 15, she continued to plan toward that goal. We decided to take a vacation for God. She was ready to serve God, but we weren't quite ready to let her go out on her own! Together we were able to experience missions with our daughter by our side, and it may well become her full-time vocation. We have been so greatly blessed by our involvement in missions and ministry. If you truly love God and want to serve Him, it seems only natural to want to give of yourself to His kingdom. God wants us to enjoy life and He grants us the desires of our heart when we are faithful to Him." □

> WHEN OUR OLDEST DAUGHTER WAS 5, WE HAD A MISSIONARY COME TO OUR HOUSE. AS SHE TURNED 10, SHE MADE A PUBLIC DECISION TO BE A MISSIONARY. AT 15, SHE CONTINUED TO PLAN TOWARD THAT GOAL.

FAMILY-TIME
REFLECTIONS

Some Practical Ideas for Families

■ **Send care packages to missionary families or ministry personnel.**
These can include toys and collectibles missionary kids can't
get overseas, certain foods or sauce mixes not locally available,
blank Christmas/birthday cards in English or other languages
as needed, office supplies, family-oriented TV series on DVD;
or ask ahead of time for a wish list.

■ **Support missionary projects that need funding to continue.**
Many missionaries are self-funded and much-needed projects
are not done due to lack of finances. Digging wells, getting
ESL materials, providing Bibles, renting facilities, purchas-
ing a scooter/motorcycle to take the gospel into remote areas,
etc., can be done if money was available.

■ **Collect and send Bibles/Bible study material/Christian
magazines/resources** (new or used) to financially strapped
churches in foreign countries.
Many churches in developing and Third-World countries simply can't buy materials to use in discipling and to teach new
believers. In some cases, workbooks are completed in pencil,
completely erased, and passed on to the next student, and so
on. Used Sunday School literature or home-group materials
are more than many churches in developing countries have
available currently.

■ **Collect eyeglasses.**
This can be a fantastic ministry that missionaries use to open
doors to share the gospel message. Sometimes it is the missionaries or ministry workers themselves who need new
glasses but can't afford them! Allowing people to see better
can change lives.

■ **Adopt orphans or help an orphanage.**
Few acts have greater immediate impact than taking care of
orphans or supporting an orphanage. Adopting an orphan

into your family will change a child's destiny and your own family's beyond imagination. Collecting clothing, school supplies, medicine, books, or sending money for food, shoes, and necessities will be an encouragement far more than you'll ever know. Loving those who have been abandoned is like ministering to Christ Himself. Even going to provide a week of Bible clubs or crafts or sports clinics will demonstrate God's love for those who have no one to hug them.

▪ **Pray.**

It seems so simple, yet few people realize how important prayer is to missionaries, orphanages, ministries, student outreach groups, churches, mission plants, Bible schools, evangelists, and more. Prayer supports all that God's people are doing wherever He has placed them. Many missionaries wait until their birthdays to make important ministry and life decisions because they know people back home are specifically praying for them on that day.

▪ **Participate in missions trips (local, in-state, international).**

Praying for others is one thing. Actually going yourself is quite another. Many people have never stepped out and gone to provide ministry or service to others. They give, pray, and encourage others, yet they have not experienced the joy of *going* and serving. Looking into the eyes of grateful people, seeing the joy and excitement children express, knowing you have made a difference in the lives of others can change your own life radically. Once you've tasted being a part of God's activity, you will not be able to get enough!

▪ **Hold food drives.**

Having to stand in line to get food for your family can be emotionally very difficult, but going there and finding there is not enough food only adds to the pain and disappointment. Most families have more than they need in their homes, and it does not take much effort to have your own food drive in your neighborhood. Many people are happy to give, and those who receive it will be so grateful they can feed their own children because you cared enough to help out.

■ **Make music in senior-care homes/hospitals.**
If you have ever seen the smiles on the faces and the joy in the eyes of seniors when children come for a visit to their senior-care facilities, you understand how easy it is to make a difference in someone's life. Do you play a musical instrument? Can your family sing a few songs? Do they know how to tell stories? If so, you are all ready to bring joy into lives that are often neglected and abandoned by family members, and left to spend the rest of their days alone.

■ **Be pen pals to missionary kids.**
With the Internet, it has never been easier to connect with people around the world. But getting an actual handwritten letter still remains an important way to touch the lives of children whose families have moved overseas to do missionary work. Getting letters lets them know they're not forgotten and that they are important, remembered, and prayed for by people in their home country.

■ **Open your home to Bible studies for kids/families.**
Few things have touched the lives of our children more than having Christians in our home on a regular basis. Our kids always loved the snacks people brought and loved talking to people who were interested in their lives and happenings. Not only does this help in discipling and encouraging other people as they spend time in God's Word together in your home, but it tells your children that your home is to be shared with others and used to encourage God's people. And we are so grateful, even indebted, to our Christian friends who have taken an interest in our children over the years.

■ **Learn to identify needs.**
Ask God to help you be more sensitive others' needs. Not everyone has the ability to sense what's going on in the lives of those around them. But asking God to help you see through His eyes will create sensitivity as His Spirit works in you and help you to see what you can do to be an encouragement to others.

■ **Be aware of resources that can meet needs.**

I (Tom) love to be a resource manager—that is, I keep my ears and eyes open to what people have or can do, and then help to match their skills or resources with those who have need of them. This helps both the needy and those who love to help others. I know people who keep a "little black book" of Christian friends who are eager to help others using the skills and resources God has given them.

■ **Honor one another in the home as a visible demonstration of Christ's lordship.**

One of the things that has caught our attention in recent days is the fact that our children's teenage friends have noticed our family is different than others. We actually sit down for meals together, are not critical or demeaning of one another, laugh together, and enjoy one another's company. The way we treat one another in our home bears witness to our relationship with God. As we demonstrate love for one another, people take notice of this love, we believe, because this is a rarity.

■ **Give Christmas presents to others.**

Christmas is certainly a great time to work and serve together as a family. Putting together gift-filled shoe boxes that are sent overseas to needy countries, singing at senior-citizen homes, writing a family newsletter together expressing the reason for the season, giving up money otherwise spent on presents and sending it to missions efforts, inviting people into your home for coffee, serving food at homeless/women's shelters, buying presents for needy children, putting together food baskets for low-income families—the opportunities seem endless.

■ **Use vacation time/money for missions trips.**

If your church does not organize family missions trips, why not begin planning now? For those who cannot afford a vacation and a missions trip, combine them! Helping others often is far more rewarding than you realize. The results of working together as a family and serving the Lord will have both immediate and long-term results in your home.

■ **Perform acts of kindness.**

Shoveling snow; chipping ice off sidewalks; putting out salt, gravel; mowing lawns—the list is extensive of what your family can do to be a blessing to others.

■ **Develop start-up companies.**

Many companies have been specifically developed as a tool for God to use in His kingdom. In other words, companies are the instruments or tools to share the gospel, support missions, employ seminary students or part-time pastors, or to demonstrate how God blesses when He is put first in business. The funny thing about these companies is that when they are given over to the Lord for His use and His purposes, He tends to bless them and use them to bring glory to Himself in the community. Is there certain expertise your family has that can be used to develop a business God can use to share the gospel or to encourage His people?

■ **Organize medical missions, agricultural missions, music missions, etc.**

Many churches organize ministries using the skills of their church members. Churches send teams each year across the globe to help train in agricultural methods, provide free medical/dental/eye-care clinics to impoverished locations, lead sports camps, provide music ministry or child care for church or missions conferences where missionaries and ministry personnel meet annually.

■ **Participate in construction projects.**

Many families band together and sign up for a variety of construction projects—build low-cost housing, repair damaged churches, renovate missionary housing, construct modest church buildings, build community playgrounds, etc.—to provide the labor on projects that bring glory to God. It is hard work, sometimes very hot and difficult, but it is a way for your whole family to work together, and it provides the workforce to complete desperately needed projects that would otherwise never be accomplished.

■ **Participate in camping ministry.**
Many campsites have little if any programming for children. There may be a lake, a playground, and volleyball net, but nothing actually organized or programmed for children. Parents often are delighted to have a safe place that provides crafts, games, snacks, and a Bible story for a few hours each day. Awana material, Vacation Bible School materials, Kid's Bible Club materials can all be modified to teach anywhere from 1 to 14 days at even remote locations. One parent teaches, the other leads singing, and all the kids help with the games and crafts. Think about safety, plan for hyperactive kids, and watch for God to do incredible things to change lives through your efforts.

Go back over the list above and check off the activities your family *could* do if God led you to.

Gaby Spicer says, "My husband, Justin, and I believe we have been entrusted with our children to teach them about God and how they can have a living relationship with Him. We have devotions with them every day and love using life's everyday opportunities to teach them about God's order, His law, His love, and His kingdom principles. We share with them about the wonders God does in our family and stand with them as we believe God for big and little things, such as trampolines, puppies, etc. Our biggest prayer is that they would love God with all their heart all the rest of their lives.... Honestly, not that they would be in ministry or be missionaries or pastors as such, but that they would just know God and know how much He loves them. We know if He has access to their heart, He will lead them in His plan for their lives." ☐

WHAT NEXT?

*I*n this book, we've examined how God chose specific families from the beginning of time to use for His purposes, has blessed and led His people, and has protected and saved His people from enemies. We've seen how, through families, He has provided a model for how His people should relate to one another and function within the church. We've looked at how the families God uses live out their devotion to God in love, service, and with an eye to the future. We've reinforced what God says about His love for and faithfulness for hurting and struggling families and individual family members. We've viewed children as a gift from God and seen through the lens of Scripture, how He uses children in significant ministry both in biblical and contemporary times. Finally, we have numerous strategies, activities, and suggestions for families to engage together with God in the work He is doing around us.

So what do you think God has in mind to do through your family? Can you see just how He has put the members of your family in place for a special purpose? The point of this book is not to make your life more complicated or busier, but to make the most of your time together as a family and as Christians.

Before you put this book down or slip it onto a shelf somewhere, please do take a moment to pray, alone and with your family members, asking God to show you His heart and what He might have in mind for your family and each member and even the future generations you influence through the legacy you leave. You might want to begin preparing now for what God might invite your family to do with Him this next year.

1. Look at the skills and gifts your family possesses.
2. Listen for what God is putting on the hearts of your family.

3. Watch for opportunities to serve the Lord.
4. Ask God's Spirit for guidance to prepare the hearts of your family for service in His kingdom.

You will be amazed at how many opportunities there are all around you for being a family of influence. May God help your family leave a legacy of faithfulness for future generations to follow. ☐

■ ■ ■

All the ends of the earth will remember and turn

to the LORD, and all the families of the nations will

bow down before him, for dominion belongs to the

LORD and he rules over the nations

(Psalm 22:27–28 NIV).

Future generations will serve him; they will

speak of the LORD to the coming generation.

People not yet born will be told:

"The LORD saved his people"

(Psalm 22:30–31 GNT).

■ ■ ■

■ ■ ■

THE FAMILY GOD USES CHALLENGE

Today we accept God's call to be a family God uses in our home, community, and wherever He may lead us. We accept the responsibility of being a family of influence in our place of work, schools, and in every area of our lives. We are determined together to leave a legacy of faithfulness for generations to come.

"As for me and my house, we will serve the LORD" (Joshua 24:15 NKJV).

Family members:

Signed _____
Date _____

Signed _____
Date _____

Signed _____
Date _____

Signed _____
Date _____

Signed _____
Date _____

Signed _____
Date _____

Group leader/pastor

Signed _____
Date _____

A FAMILY COMMISSIONING SERVICE

(This is a suggested outline for a brief commissioning service that can be held during a time of corporate church worship. It is meant to bring a focus on families who are serving the Lord together, but can also be used for others who represent your church by serving God faithfully in their community or around the world.)

1. **SAY:** Today we want to take a few moments in our service to recognize and pray for those in our church family who have committed their lives to serving the Lord together as families. God calls each one of us to serve Him in various ways, but we do not always formally acknowledge those who are fighting the spiritual battles by representing our church in the community. We hope that today each person will take time to reflect on how God may be asking each of us to join Him in His kingdom work and make a personal commitment to serve Him as well.

2. Have each family/person that accepts *The Family God Uses* challenge come to the front of the church.

3. **SAY:** These families standing before you have accepted God's Great Commission challenge to go into the world knowing that as Christ said, "All authority has been given to Me in heaven and on earth. Go therefore and make disciples of all the nations, baptizing them in the name of the Father and of the Son and of the Holy Spirit, teaching them to observe all things that I have commanded you; and lo, I am with you always, even to the end of the age" (Matthew 28:18–20 NKJV). They have also accepted the challenge of Joshua: "As for me and my house, we will serve the LORD" (Joshua 24:15 NKJV).

❑ Our church believes that every person has been called by God into His service to use his or her spiritual gifts and talents in kingdom work.

❏ We believe that God strategically places each person and each family so that He can use them in unique and significant ways to have an impact on the lives of people around them.

❏ We believe families cannot accomplish God-sized tasks on their own and need the full support, encouragement, and equipping of a whole church family.

Today, we want to stop and pray for these families, asking God to guide, protect, and help them do what He has asked them to do so that together we can rejoice in what God accomplishes through them to change lives for eternity.

4. **PRAY:** Father, You created these families. You placed each member in them on purpose. You knew the struggles, the victories, the challenges, and the successes they would have as they established their homes and grew in their love and support for one another. They have committed their lives to You and asked You to be a part of their homes. They have given their homes to You for Your use and now commit to Your service where You have placed them and where You are calling them to serve You. We don't know the challenges they will face, but You do. You brought them to be a part of our church family and so we commit this day to pray for them, to support them, to encourage them, and to help them in whatever way we can as they represent our church family in the community and as they serve You in Your kingdom work. May they each come to know You more personally and may their love for You deepen as they work together to seek and to serve You. May You receive all the glory. In the name of Jesus Christ we pray. Amen.

5. **PRESENT:** Give each family an "As for me and my house, we will serve the LORD" certificate signed by the pastor and staff and a family devotional book (such as *Experiencing God Day by Day* or *Called and Accountable*). ☐

■ ■ ■

RECOMMENDED RESOURCES

Blackaby, Henry, Richard Blackaby, and Claude King. *Experiencing God: Knowing and Doing the Will of God.* Nashville: LifeWay Church Resources, 2007.

Blackaby, Henry, and Tom Blackaby. *Anointed to Be God's Servants: How God Blesses Those Who Serve Together.* Nashville: Thomas Nelson Publishers, 2006.

Blackaby, Henry T., and Melvin D. Blackaby. *A God Centered Church: Experiencing God Together.* Nashville: B&H Publishing Group, 2007.

Blackaby, Richard. *Putting a Face on Grace: Living a Life Worth Passing On.* Sisters, OR: Multnomah Publishers, 2006.

Blackaby, Richard. *Unlimiting God: Increasing Your Capacity to Experience the Divine.* Colorado Springs: Multnomah Books, 2008.

Blackaby, Tom, and Kim Blackaby. *The Family God Uses: Becoming a Home of Influence.* Workbook for small groups or families. Nashville: LifeWay Church Resources, 2009.

_____. *The Family God Uses: Leaving a Legacy of Influence.* Hardcover. Birmingham, AL: New Hope Publishers, 2009.

Holmen, Mark A. *Building Faith at Home: Why Faith at Home Must Be Your Church's #1 Priority.* Ventura, CA: Regal Books, 2007.

Milne, Bruce. *Dynamic Diversity: Bridging Class, Age, Race and Gender in the Church.* Downers Grove, IL: InterVarsity Press, 2007.

Omartian, Stormie. *The Power of a Praying Parent*. Eugene, OR: Harvest House Publishers, 2007.

_____. *The Power of a Praying Husband*. Eugene, OR: Harvest House Publishers, 2001.

Osborne, Rick. *801 Questions Children Ask About God with Answers from the Bible*. Carol Stream, IL: Tyndale House Publishers, Inc., 2000.

Osborne, Rick. *The Singing Bible: A 52 Song Journey Through the Bible*. A Lightwave Publishing Production, Inc., 1993.

Osborne, Rick. *Partnering with Parents: Putting Churches and Families in a Biblical Partnership for the Progressive, Moral and Spiritual Development of Children*. Sunday School curriculum. Release date 2010.

(The above mentioned resources and other parenting resources by Rick Osborne are available at www.ChristianParentingDaily.com; http://rick-osborne.com; or http://rick-osborne.com/category/resources-for-parents/.)

Trent, John, PhD, Rick Osborne, and Kurt Bruner, gen. eds. *Parents' Guide to the Spiritual Growth of Children: Helping Your Children Develop a Personal Faith*. Carol Stream, IL: Tyndale House Publishers, Inc., 2003.

Waldrep, Phil. *Parenting Prodigals: Six Principles for Bringing Your Son or Daughter Back to God*. Friendswood, TX: Baxter Press, 2001.

Whitney, Donald S. *Family Worship: in the Bible, in History & in Your Home*. Shepherdsville, KY: Center for Biblical Spirituality, 2006.

■ ■ ■

ORGANIZATIONS AND MINISTRIES WHERE FAMILIES CAN SERVE OR FIND MISSIONS OPPORTUNITIES

Union Gospel Mission

Union Gospel Mission is a Christian ministry dedicated to meeting the spiritual, social, and physical needs of people. Your involvement can help change more lives by restoring hope. As a community, it's important to build each other up and give back. Located in several cities throughout North America; e.g., Seattle (www.ugm.org); Vancouver (www.ugm.ca); Twin Cities (www.ugmtc.org).

The Salvation Army

An international movement, the Salvation Army is an integral part of the universal Christian church. Its message is based on the Bible. Its ministry is motivated by the love of God. Its mission is to preach the gospel of Jesus Christ and to meet human needs in His name without discrimination. (www.salvationarmy.org)

North American Mission Board

Families on Mission is a prepackaged, weeklong (Saturday through Thursday) family missions opportunity that allows Mom, Dad, and grandparents to model an on-mission lifestyle for their children and grandchildren. Parents and grandparents have the unique privilege to be "hands-on" as they guide their family through devotions, missions awareness, missions projects, worship, family small-group discussions, and interaction with resident missionaries and the community. Missions activities include acts of kindness and other evangelism events, light construction and painting, yard work, prayerwalking, Vacation Bible School, sports camps, block parties, and others. Phone: 1-800-462-8657, ext. 6456 (www.namb.net)

International Mission Board

The main objective of the International Mission Board is

presenting the gospel of Jesus Christ in order to lead individuals to saving faith in Him and result in church-planting movements among all the peoples of the world. Specific opportunities for families as volunteers: http://going.imb.org/volunteers/Step_1/family.asp.

OPERATION MOBILIZATION

Operation Mobilization (OM) works in more than 100 countries, motivating and equipping people to share God's love with people all over the world. OM seeks to help plant and strengthen churches, especially in areas of the world where Christ is least known. Each short-term missions project listed shows whether or not they are "family friendly." (www.om.org)

SHORTTERMMISSIONS.COM

This Web site exists to help people quickly connect with missions opportunities that fit their gifts and calling. Its goals are to become a central place for people to learn about, interact on, and discover short-term missions trips; and to provide an effective way for organizations to get the word out about their missions opportunities. They desire for people to discover opportunities for using their unique set of experiences, gifts, and passions for advancing God's kingdom. (www.shorttermmissions.com)

ADVENTURES IN MISSIONS

Adventures in Missions (AIM) is an interdenominational missions organization that focuses on discipling. It emphasizes prayer and relationships in its work among the poor. In the 17 years since AIM was established, it has taken 65,000 people to the missions field, some for a year or longer. Through 14 bases around the world, it provides year-round ministry to places where "the least of these" are found. AIM believes that by giving people the opportunity to hold orphans, bring hope to the hopeless, and pray for the sick, lives are transformed. It seeks to disciple as Jesus did. Its vision is that God would use it to raise up a generation of radically committed disciples of Jesus Christ! (www.adventures.org)

SEND

SEND is an interdenominational faith missions agency with more than 600 missionaries in more than 20 countries of Asia, Europe, and North America. For more than 50 years they have been...starting churches where there are none by evangelizing the unreached, nurturing disciples, and developing leaders from among the national people. Can accommodate families but not specifically oriented to do so. (www.send.org)

WOMAN'S MISSIONARY UNION*

Woman's Missionary Union* (WMU*) is a nonprofit organization that offers an array of missions resources including conferences, ministry ideas and models, volunteer opportunities, curriculum for age-level organizations, leadership training, books, and more. (Phone: 1-800-968-7301, www.wmu.com)

WMU Events aimed at families and children include:

FamilyFEST℠

(http://www.wmu.com/VolunteerConnection) is a prepackaged missions trip for families, adult teams, and student teams. Ministry driven, this annual event includes hands-on ministry projects, pre–missions trip training, and more.

Children's Ministry Day®

(http://www.childrensmissions.com) each year provides opportunities for children's involvement in an assortment of missions projects.

Trade publisher New Hope Publishers®

(www.newhopepublishers.com) provides resources that challenge Christian believers to understand and be radically involved in God's mission. Some of its missional resources include:
Called and Accountable: Discovering Your Place in God's Eternal Purpose
Faces in the Crowd: Reaching Your International Neighbor for Christ
Zowie! 200+ Ministries Kids Can Do

Setting Up Stones: A Parent's Guide to Making Your Home a Place
   of Worship
Missions Moments 2
Families on Mission

WorldCrafts℠ parties give families the opportunity to join in simple to elaborate events that benefit some of the world's poorest communities. Learn more about the Set1Free campaign to support artisan groups working with those at high risk of exploitation. Artisan stories, prayer resources, and more are available at www.WorldCraftsVillage.com.

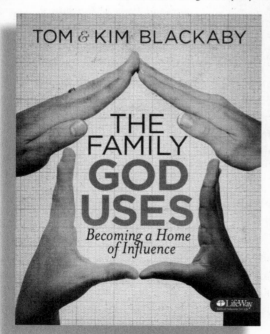

Other New Hope Books
by the Blackaby Family

**Called & Accountable
52-Week Devotional**
*Discovering Your Place
in God's Eternal Purpose*
**Henry and Norman Blackaby,
with Dana Blackaby**
ISBN-10: 1-59669-214-6
ISBN-13: 978-1-59669-214-5

Called and Accountable
*Discovering Your Place
in God's Eternal Purpose*
**Henry T. Blackaby and Norman
Blackaby**
ISBN-10: 1-59669-047-X
ISBN-13: 978-1-59669-047-9

Called and Accountable
*Discovering Your Place
in God's Eternal Purpose*
**Henry T. Blackaby and
Norman C. Blackaby**
ISBN-10: 1-56309-946-2
ISBN-13: 978-1-56309-946-5

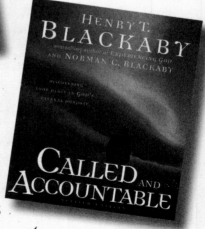

Available in bookstores everywhere.

For information about these books or any New Hope product,
visit www.newhopepublishers.com.